Loving Again

A Guide to Online Dating for Widows and Widowers

By Gail Decker Cushman
and Robert L. Mitchell

Copyright 2023

Copyright © 2023 Gail Decker Cushman

All rights reserved. No part of this book may be reproduced or used in any manner without written permission of the copyright owner except for the use of quotations in a book review.

Edited by AnnaMarie McHargue and Anita Stephens

Designed by Eric Hendrickson

ISBN (paperback): 978-1-7376288-9-7

ISBN (ebook): 979-8-9895968-0-5

www.gailcushman.com

DEDICATION:

To the many widows and widowers
Who hear the sounds of silence every day
Who understand what emptiness and loneliness mean
Who wonder if there is something better.
Break out your old dancing shoes
And step out on the floor!

*Life should not be a journey to the grave
with the intention of arriving safely in a pretty
and well-preserved body,
but rather to skid in broadside in a cloud of smoke,
thoroughly used up, totally worn out,
and loudly proclaiming,
Wow! What a Ride!*

Hunter S. Thompson, American Journalist

AUTHORS' NOTES

We write this book about our experiences and what we learned as we embarked on our romantic journey. We do not claim to be experts, rather we offer our observations and experiences to demonstrate how exciting, fun, and life-changing December romances can be if you are willing to take a chance.

Online dating is sometimes given a bad reputation, and it carries risk along with considerable rewards, but we seniors have common sense, experience, and knowledge of a lifetime to sort and predict outcomes. You alone can decide what is on your dance card. It could be the tango or the bunny-hop, and you can join this challenging way of meeting new people if you pick up that dance card and hit "send" on your magic keyboard.

We make no promises or guarantees through using this book. Be as careful with your heart as you are with your head and your pocketbook. Our best advice is to be brave yet use your experience and common sense and be careful. Happy dating!

TABLE OF CONTENTS

Preface	An Unlikely Love Story	1
Chapter 1	Losing Your Dancing Partner	3
Chapter 2	Picking Up the Pieces	6
Chapter 3	Loneliness, an Invisible Disease	15
Chapter 4	Should I Throw Away My Knitting and Buy New Dancing Shoes?	23
Chapter 5	Dating: You Must Be Kidding	34
Chapter 6	Dating: The Demographics of Senior Dating	45
Chapter 7	Hey, Good-Lookin'!	48
Chapter 8	Taking It Slow and Easy	52
Chapter 9	But Wait! What Is Grandma Up to Now?	63
Chapter 10	Internet Dating: A New Sock Hop	70
Chapter 11	Strut Your Stuff	80
Chapter 12	The Eight-Thousand-Site Question	90
Chapter 13	What a Hunk, but Who Is This Person?	116

Chapter 14	The First Date Adventure	126
Chapter 15	Slow Dance, Romance	133
Chapter 16	SEX: Now That I've Captured Your Attention	139
Chapter 17	Getting on with the Rhythm of Life	150
Chapter 18	Online Dating Glossary	158
Chapter 19	Play-by-Play Book	167
Chapter 20	Let's Go Hunting: A Workbook	173
Works Cited		185
About the Authors		189

PREFACE

An Unlikely Love Story

LOVE!

Oh, my gosh…I'm seventy-six years old and twelve months a widow and now somebody I don't know has asked me for a date…

This is a love story, as unlikely a love story as you will ever find, a love between two people, seeking and finding adventure, excitement, and the passion of young love, not at age twenty or fifty, but rekindled later in life, beyond three quarters of a century. Our love story is of two people who each were happily married, deeply loving one person, sharing a full and good life for 40 to 50 years and suddenly left alone as death and grieving smashed our lives. This is the true story of us picking up the pieces, deciding to get on with the adventure of life, meeting and falling in love through the Internet. Both widowed, Robert and Gail had loved their spouses without question, yet fell in love again with each other, a new person, a new life, a new adventure. They lived in two different states, with dissimilar backgrounds, an educator and a rancher, city and country, a Lexus and a Ford pickup with a trailer hitch. They both loved travel and the thrill of discovering and exploring new things, and somehow, they were able to bond to each other's soul. (How corny does that sound?)

LOVING AGAIN

They wrote this book about chasing love, dating again, using the Internet, and becoming excited about the touch of a new love. They learned that their hearts had room for a second person, a new person to love deeply and completely. Their tale of romance includes how they navigated living six hundred miles apart, how their families coped (or didn't), and how laughter entered their life again. This book is a guide to all those silver-haired foxes and vixens seeking new life after the ultimate loss and is a roadmap of romance and love for the boomer generation who want to jitterbug on the internet dance floor.

Life dealt many blows to Robert and Gail as they both struggled to recover from the emotional desert left after their long-time loves had passed on after suffering through lengthy illnesses that necessitated caregiving and sacrifice. The loss of their spouses devastated them and they saw no hope until they picked themselves up and hesitantly embarked on a journey of finding new friendship, new romance, and, yes, love. They put safety concerns in place, and moved forward, bold, yet cautious. After all, these folks were tough, raised in the Nuclear Age, practicing hiding-under-your-desk refuge from nuclear attack during their elementary school days. They lived through sixty years of social change, paying bills, and now the frustrating Age of the Password. They did it all.

Love. Can one fall in love for a second time? Yup, they did and what a jolt it was, the touch of her hand, his smile, and the nightly pillow talks about nothing and everything.

CHAPTER 1

Losing Your Dancing Partner

Oh, my gosh...I'm seventy-six years old and twelve months a widow, and now somebody I don't know has asked me for a date—an online date—but I barely even know what that is. I was Tom's wife for over half a century, but that life has passed, and it's finally sunk in that he's not coming back, quick person that I am. I'm about to enter a dating site. How did I get here?

He died, but I didn't, that's how I got here. I didn't really have a choice in my current situation because Tom, the love of my life, to whom I was married for over fifty years, died. And now, he's gone and I'm still here, healthy and active, wanting to complete our bucket list by continuing to have adventures and living my life out. I always thought I was a good problem solver, but this problem had dropped itself squarely in my lap, and suddenly I feel like a woman without a country. What do I do? Where do I go? I thought about it a lot, and I saw only one solution: status quo, being a lonely widow for the rest of my life.

This book tells the story of the difficult journey of losing a spouse and dealing with the sounds of an empty house, no matter how loudly you set the CD player or TV volume. It relates the tales of Robert and Gail, both widowers over the age of seventy-five who lived through the life-changing event of losing a longtime spouse, struggling with the decisions that had to be made. Stay the course, alter the direction, or choose something totally different.

Although losing someone you love happens in every family, it is different for all of us and leaves an empty space needing to be filled by activities, people, or change. Sometimes an accident or sudden illness leaves a blank space immediately: right here and right now, allowing no time for preparation or adjustment. No goodbyes, no last-minute kisses, nothing. He or she just doesn't come home from work one day or doesn't wake up or a different type of tragedy, such as murder or suicide, that is difficult and impossible to talk about.

For others the ordeal of the death experience may take a couple of years or even longer, and the surviving spouse switches roles from spouse to caregiver. Many of us serve as caregivers when one spouse is diagnosed with an extended illness, changing our roles as spouse to that of a very special personal nurse. We all understood the "until death do us part" promise but did not ever think it would happen to us, and the months spent watching our love pass away take a dreadful emotional toll. One spouse becomes dependent on his or her mate for many things, health issues, transportation, bathing, economics, and more. The time spent during these months allows time for asking the unasked questions such as "Who gets your jewelry?" or "Do you want to be cremated or be buried in the ground?" or "Where did you put the title to the car?" or a common problem for widows, "Could you show me how to run the remote?" Talking about imminent death is always uncomfortable, and all too often, these questions lie incomplete, even after several years. The surviving spouse is left wondering the answers, with no one to ask. Each chemo treatment or new drug promises hope, and the nurses pat your hand, offering weak and sometimes insincere smiles for the surviving spouse, who knows and fears this terminal illness with only one outlet.

Losing Your Dancing Partner

Unexpressed words and feelings linger in our minds, and we regret the unspoken and undone, like not giving one more compliment, offering a flirty wink, or simply saying another "I love you" when he or she walked out the door. On the other hand, we may regret the spoken or done, like words voiced in anger or slamming the door or throwing something across the room because it wasn't in the right place. Important questions that we should have asked lie in the back of our minds. We didn't ask because after all, we could ask them tomorrow. Only now, time has run out and no tomorrow will appear to resolve these and other questions. Our unopened emotional baggage—like fuming over an unresolved issue that occurred years ago, an epithet blurted out in a moment of frustration, being too tired for a last opportunity for lovemaking, or an unresolved argument about nothing important, such as leaving dirty clothes on the floor or an unpaid bill—hovers over us. These memories of lost opportunity can cause even more regret and grief. What's done is done and reparations are too late.

We anticipate what it will be like, yet it is difficult to impossible to prepare for. Selfishly, we may consider only ourselves, but when a death occurs, it is important to realize that many are affected. Children lose their parents, coworkers lose their mentors, brothers and sisters lose their siblings, and sometimes parents lose their children. The moment a person dies, the finality of a relationship crashes down. The minute that a spouse is announced dead, it hits us like a hammer. The "until death do us part" promise has happened and now what's next?

CHAPTER 2

Picking Up the Pieces

Our story is of two people who each were happily married, deeply loving one person, sharing a full and good life forty to fifty years, and suddenly left alone as death and grieving smashed our lives. This is the true story of us picking up the pieces, deciding to get on with the adventure of life, meeting and falling in love through the Internet. Both widowed, Robert and Gail had loved their spouses without question, yet fell in love again with each other, a new person, a new life, a new adventure. They had never met, never even heard of each other because they lived in two different states, with dissimilar backgrounds, an educator and a rancher, city and country, a Lexus and a Ford pickup with a trailer hitch. They both loved travel and the thrill of discovering and exploring new things, and somehow, they were able to bond to each other's soul. (How corny does that sound?)

They wrote this book about chasing love, dating again, using the Internet, and becoming excited about the touch of a new love. They learned that their hearts had room for a second person, a new person to love deeply and completely. Their tale of romance includes how they navigated living six hundred miles apart, how their families coped (or didn't), and how laughter entered their life again. This book is a guide to all those seeking new life after the ultimate loss and is a road map of romance and love for the boomer generation who want to jitterbug on the Internet dance floor.

Picking Up the Pieces

❧ *Gail's Story* ☙

Tom had been in the VA nursing home for over a year, and every day I would drive to see him and cry all the way home. We didn't talk much during those two years about what the future held for me, and we both knew, but didn't admit, what was in store for him. We had seen lawyers, doctors, accountants, and the VA, and we had made all the recommended arrangements when the doctors first diagnosed his five diseases, and nothing had changed except that he became weaker, losing more and more strength and interest in life, becoming so ill that I could not care for him without help. My daily visits somewhat cheered both of us up, but we both knew what was coming. We had traveled extensively and continued talking about the people we had met and experiences we had and added our dreams of new travel during the next few years, although we both knew that our plans would lie fallow, never to be completed. If our dreams were to come to fruition, they would become my dreams, and only his memory would be a part of them.

After a few months I envisioned him as a complicated jigsaw puzzle, and as I left the nursing home each day, I felt a small piece of him had gone missing. And then one day, nearly two years later, the man I had been married to for 51.8 years disappeared, poof, every piece of him had evaporated into thin air, but he was still breathing. It was one of the most difficult weeks of my life. Shortly afterward, he stopped breathing.

The three weeks that followed, after his demise, were filled with a whirlwind of activity. Family and friends called and sent cards and dutifully repeated the words, "My condolences," "I'm so sorry," or "If I can do anything, don't hesitate to ask." But in the end, they were words, just words, and hearing them didn't make a dent in the heartbreak that I felt.

LOVING AGAIN

We were dealing with Covid 19 and all the restrictions it carried with it, including masks everywhere, but things had to be done, and in the weeks that followed, I began completing all the requisite things, contacting Social Security, changing automobile titles, notifying various credit card companies, and sorting his clothes. I filled boxes of mementos for our grandchildren, who looked at me puzzled as I handed off containers of jewelry, socks, and his array of ties and wool sweaters, also not something they wanted. I watched TV and continued to write, but mostly I lived alone with my thoughts in a chasm of silence, even while the TV blasted away. I thought of our journey, one through faith, jobs, family, and even our series of pets. I felt odd, both happy and sad. Happy that he was no longer suffering and sad because I didn't see anything in my future.

The day that he died and left the VA nursing home was an interesting day. My kids accompanied me to the nursing home, where a crowd of people waited for a Marine sergeant to play "Taps" as they carried him from the building. We had a tearful, quick lunch, then parted ways, and I returned home, expecting things to be the same as they had for the two years that he had been at the VA nursing home, quiet and empty, but they weren't. Something was different, unidentifiable, but different. While he was still alive, I constantly felt his presence, an aura as I saw his chair, his books, his favorite holey sweater. During those days I knew he was still a part of me, eager to do something, something fun, eating dinner or watching his beloved Florida Gators. I thought that maybe a miracle would happen, and he would be released, hale and healthy, as he had been a dozen years before.

Something had changed. Was it my house or was it I who had changed? He had disappeared. I no longer saw his chair; rather I saw his chair without him. I no longer saw his books, rather clutter that needed to be straightened and cleaned. His favorite sweater didn't look the same either. It had grown old and ratty, and I didn't have the heart to put it in the trash, so that afternoon I took it to the resale shop and let them deal with it.

Night fell and I decided it was time to go to bed, and this is kind of spooky, but true. Our bedspread was a deep burgundy, which I had neatly made before I had gone to the nursing home to hear "Taps." That day, in the middle of the bed was a tiny heart, like one that had been cut with a paper punch, a tiny white paper heart. I owned a lot of office supplies but no paper punches, so to this day, I do not know where it came from. I taped it to the base of my computer, reminding me that some things are inexplainable. We had not understood the whys of his illness and death, and now somehow, someone joined me in my grief.

We delayed the funeral for three weeks, time for family to come from the East Coast. The day of the funeral is a blur, except that a lot of people greeted me and my family. I remember the Marine who handed me the folded flag saying, "The United States of America thanks Captain Cushman for his service," which felt like slamming the door on the coffin. It was final; he was dead, buried, and would never return.

I returned from the funeral and walked into an empty house, searching for something to do. For the first few months after his passing, his presence wavered. Sometimes he was watching me, other times, not. I swapped out the time I had spent visiting him with baking cookies and bread and gave them to my friends and family, who, of course, didn't want them. I wrote books and blogs, which helped keep me upbeat. I cleaned, but with only one person living here, how dirty could it get? I thought about getting a dog for company, but I still hoped to travel, and I didn't think it was good to leave a pet for weeks at a time. Maybe later.

While the first few weeks were filled with sympathy cards and notes, the constant din of friends reaching out turned to silence. The phone didn't ring, the cards stopped coming, and my friends stopped calling.

Loving Again

I felt like I had suddenly become a marked person, turned into some sort of pariah of death. When I called my friends, they asked what I was doing, but not how I was doing, and the calls grew fewer and farther between, shorter and shorter. One day I called a friend and tossed out the idea of going to lunch, as we had many times before. She answered my question with a question, asking if I enjoyed the lasagna she had made after the funeral, and had I finished it, which made me wonder if she meant her lasagna to replace our lunch dates.

I attended a couple of grief groups but didn't find comfort in listening to others' sad, often tragic, stories, and how they coped. I began to accept being on my own, thrown into a silent world. I wanted conversation but found myself talking to myself, and I began to look forward to shopping because, surely, I would run into someone who wanted a conversation. Many stores had switched from clerks to self-service, so even going shopping didn't help much. I played dumb and pretended to be unable to work the check-out machines, just to have someone to talk with. One time the aisle ran out of plastic bags, and what luck! I got to have an extended conversation while the clerk replenished the supply. Before long I began to relish the thought of visiting with the people who worked at Cabela's or Costco. Soon I was on a first-name basis with the store's staff but found it a faulty idea because my credit card balance began bulging as I lurked around the fishing and hunting equipment or sampling the tasty pot stickers. Maybe those people were widowed too, and this was their way of coping. I thought about applying for a job at one of the big-box stores but decided I wasn't that desperate. Or maybe I was. Desperate times call for desperate measures.

PICKING UP THE PIECES

❧ *Robert's Story* ❧

Patty is gone. My wife, my lover, and most of all my friend has left me. She was my rock through business deals, moving across the country, running a ranch, and raising a family. We worked and played together for forty-two years, but after two years of battling cancer, she passed away the first part of December, leaving me alone. It wasn't something either of us planned, but it happened, and I was left with a new role to play, that of widower, bereaved husband.

Social scientists say grief has five stages:

Denial   Anger   Bargaining   Depression   Acceptance

I found these true, but as caregiver of a terminally ill spouse, Patty and I had talked through these grief stages time and again and absorbed and dealt with denial and anger months before. Every day of her illness, her cancer stole a piece of her, and after she died, I felt some of me had been stolen too, making me feel more alone than I already was. I had no one to bargain with except God, but I had a strong faith, and He gave me the strength to deal with my inner turmoil. I found I needed a way to keep myself together, to remove the depression and self-pity. Although I didn't think I felt sorry for myself, in hindsight, I probably did. Loneliness can manifest itself as depression or self-pity, and I had plenty of both. The colors of life turned gray, and at times blackness seemed to descend like a curtain over me. I wanted to cry or yell, but my voice was paralyzed. Somehow the link between my wanting to act and the brain censoring anything resembling feelings resulted in nothingness. The indescribable sounds of silence boomed in my brain and overwhelmed me like waves crashing onto the rocks. In this swirling dark backwater, I was dulling down. I found solace in the everyday tasks of life, and gradually those regimented make-work tasks gave me a handhold like a rock climber, and I started moving upward. My mind was active, but I couldn't find the energy or stamina to get on with life. I had not drunk alcohol in years, didn't smoke and wasn't about to start, but fell into the mindless habit of watching hour after hour of TV because I had nothing else to do.

Immediately after her funeral, well-wishers, cards, letters, and emails flooded my email, phone, and mailbox, all expressing their condolences. My neighbors showered me with food, and life became almost too busy, too full, but after a couple of weeks, these personal interactions slowed, leaving me alone with my dog, Cody, and the continuing sounds of silence. Someone recommended grief counseling, and I made an honest effort, but it didn't help. I talked with my friends at church, but still, I found my life empty and without purpose. My doorbell stopped ringing, and the flood of cards, plates of cookies, letters, and emails slowed to a drizzle, which was a good thing because I was packing on the pounds. Even when I spoke with my friends and family, they seemed distant, as if afraid of getting too close. She died in early December, and surprisingly, I spent Christmas and New Year's Day in front of the TV, alone. On a whim, I called three of my closest friends, but they cut the conversation short, and I wondered if they thought death might be catching. The laughter in the background reinforced my loneliness. As I continued contacting family and friends, my calls seemed to interrupt their lives, and their conversations grew shorter. After all, what could they say that hadn't already been said?

The weather in Montana is cold, and the frozen ground caused us to delay Patty's graveside service until spring. As these four and a half months passed, I began to find my way, and managing this service helped the days to pass quickly. I am good at managing, and my brain began to click again. The funeral in our church in December had been formal, lots of eulogies and hugs, crying and handshakes, but the graveside service was informal on purpose. People talk of celebration of life and *maybe I can relate, but I think that term is trite. This was a gathering to do a job, bury a wife, a mother, a grandmother, and friend with all of us taking part and to remember her. We held it on her birthday in April, and I applied all my organizational skills to bring my adult grandkids into the actual work of burying their grandmother, hoping it would help bring closure to all of us. What I did not realize was that preparing for her graveside service snapped me out of my self-pity and drew my grandchildren closer to me.*

A week before the graveside service, my grandson brought over his backhoe, and I used it to dig her grave. Afterward, my grandson helped load the backhoe, and we returned to town to have a beer and discuss how this would all work.

We pulled up to the local restaurant in our pickups with the backhoe sitting on my grandson's trailer, walked into the bar with mud on our boots and overalls, and joined a group of manly men sitting at the bar watching NASCAR on the television. I felt relaxed and better than I had in months and ordered a non-alcoholic beer. Before it arrived, my grandson said, "Grandpa, we need to talk."

I wondered what he meant, fearing he would want me to sell my house and send me to a retirement home, but I took a deep breath and said, "Sure."

What happened next was almost out of a soap opera. He put his hand on my shoulder and said, "Grandpa, you need to stop feeling sorry for yourself and get on with life. You have too much life left to sit out the rest of your life, waiting to die." My smile turned to a frown, and I asked what he meant. He grinned and said, "Date. Start dating. I have talked to my brothers and cousins, and we think you need to get out there. See women."

"Get out there? Where?" I asked, still thinking he was going to move me out of my comfortable home to somewhere I didn't want to go.

LOVING AGAIN

"*Online dating is the cool thing for single people now. Try it out. You have a computer and know how to use the Internet. You always told us life is an adventure.*"

Simultaneously I had an ah-ha moment yet felt I had been kicked by a mule and shook my head. He was right, but I hadn't seen it until he said it. I said I would try, but cautioned, "What about all the bad things you hear regarding Internet dating, you know, Dr. Phil and Oprah? They say it's dangerous, and Grandma just died. It might be too soon, and I don't think I can do it."

He laughed and said, "*You'll figure it out, Grandpa, you're pretty smart, and Grandma told us she wanted you to get on with life. We think this is what she wanted.*" He took one last bite of his burger, rose, and said, "Call me," as I watched him leave the bar with the backhoe behind his truck.

I finished my drink, paid the bill, and returned to my home. Over the next week, I thought about what he had said and mulled over the events of that day. The graveside service at the little country church went well, my grandkids all doing their part. The family somewhat came together, and now I realized I needed to move on. I felt closure and peace and resolved that I needed to do something. My grandson had suggested online dating. Maybe…

CHAPTER 3

LONELINESS, AN INVISIBLE DISEASE

Now widowed, we ask ourselves, "My life has changed, but what am I missing?" We can write a laundry list of things we miss, different for everyone, with the most common being "I don't have conversations anymore." Living alone means our day-to-day conversation stands still or doesn't happen, breeding isolation and solitude. Phone calls and visits are fewer and farther between, and since friends are aging, they may be suffering the same loneliness and depression as we are.

Conversation is the basis for getting and giving information but also expressing emotions such as joy, anger, confusion, and random thoughts, and when it disappears, our brains become less active. Loneliness can cause a breakdown in our whole social system.

Loneliness comes in a lot of forms. Feeling sad or sorry for yourself when no one calls or comes to visit is only one. Loneliness is devastating, even deadly, which is how it has become a subject studied closely by schools and medical institutions. Loneliness for a widowed person may be an invisible disease, not recognizable by family, friends, or even the medical community. Even more frustrating is that a lonely individual doesn't necessarily see their feelings and actions as caused by being lonely.

Those who have studied it have come up with a list of identifiers. In the "Power of Positivity," published in December 2022, we see the following cautions:

"1. ANGER AND IRRITABILITY: When people report symptoms of depression, these symptoms are often coupled with feelings of resentment, anger, irritability, and even periods of violence. If these feelings go unattended, patterns of passive-aggressive behavior develop, and it becomes difficult to manage. It is helpful to discuss feelings of anger and aggression with a counselor who is trained to help you find healthy ways to express these emotions without damaging your relationships.

2. SELF-CRITICISM: Although we all have an inner critic that is fairly easy to silence for most of us, people that suffer from loneliness and depression find it incredibly hard to silence this negative inner influence. This pattern of "stinking thinking" becomes a downward spiral that just exacerbates other self-destructive behaviors. Pay attention to your own self-talk and notice if you lean toward the positive or negative. Learn to combat negative, judgmental thoughts with positive self-talk, and your mood will improve.

3. FEELINGS OF HOPELESSNESS: People suffering from depression often report that one of the most debilitating emotions that they experience is feeling hopeless. In extreme cases, people can feel like their symptoms will never subside, causing some to seek to end their lives. Small steps can help you begin to climb out of the hole that these feelings cause. Importantly, experiencing little successes in relationships and in life will, over time, reduce these feelings and provide emotional relief.

4. LOSS OF INTEREST IN RELATIONSHIPS AND LIFE IN GENERAL: When people suffer from depression, they lose interest in things that they used to enjoy. Suddenly, things like going to movies, enjoying time spent with family and friends, and even participating in recreational activities become mundane and uninteresting. People who suffer from depression

develop an aversion to keeping up their social lives, which can contribute to feelings of isolation and loneliness. This becomes a vicious cycle that perpetuates itself if help is not offered. Recognizing this symptom and then reaching out for help and support is key to breaking the cycle.

5. CHANGES IN WEIGHT AND APPEARANCE: Many people suffering from depression lose interest in food, which can contribute to significant weight loss. Others suffering from depression eat to excess in an attempt to make themselves feel better. Of course, this produces the undesirable effect of weight gain and poor health. Focusing on eating healthy, nutrition-rich foods that stimulate brain cell development will alleviate and reduce depressive symptoms.

6. CHANGES IN SLEEPING HABITS: According to recent studies, nearly three-fourths of people suffering from depression also suffer from insomnia. Fear, anxiety, and the inability to "switch off" anxious thoughts contribute to feelings of frustration and hopelessness. These not only disturb sufferers during the day but also affect normal sleep and rest patterns. Many patients try to compensate by adopting irregular sleep patterns or consuming caffeine to excess, which does not allow the body to adopt its natural circadian rhythms. It is important to find things that help you relax at night. Also, realize that as you treat your symptoms, you will eventually feel better about your sleep cycle.

7. FATIGUE: Because you may not be getting the restorative sleep that you need, you will most likely experience fatigue at some point during your day. Depressed bodies are in a constant state of stress. It can be exhausting to try to recover your energy and balance your system while under mental and emotional duress.

8. UNEXPLAINED ACHES AND PAINS: A common complaint of people suffering from depression is that they experience generalized aches and pains. Neurotransmitters such as serotonin and norepinephrine not only influence mood but many biochemical processes in the body as well.

When these natural chemicals are blocked in your brain, it can result in a heightened experience of pain. With a tendency to indulge in negative thinking, pain can be perceived as more severe than it actually is.

Final Thoughts: Acknowledge Your Struggle; There Is Help Available

In order to overcome loneliness and depression, you must first acknowledge that there is a problem. Importantly, embrace your opportunities for assistance. Then, surround yourself with loving and caring people who want to support you as you learn to restore your mental, emotional, and physical health."

Accordingly, one may deduce that loneliness creates fertile ground for negative thinking, even depression. A 2023 study published in *Nature Aging* even suggests that negative thoughts, including those symptoms of anxiety and depression, speed up brain aging. In addition, remaining in that same negative emotional state leads to a higher risk of depression. A 2020 study published in the journal *Alzheimer's & Dementia* links depression, including repetitive negative thinking (RNT), to dementia.

Widowed persons try to be strong people, not breaking down because of the death of their spouse. "I can handle this." They may try to think happy thoughts and attempt to exhibit happiness and positivity on the outside, while their heart is breaking on the inside, not only from the death of their spouse, but from being alone, not having a soul mate. Pearl Buck wisely said, "The person who tries to live alone will not succeed as a human being. His heart withers if it does not answer another heart. His mind shrinks away if he hears only the echoes of his own thoughts and finds no other inspiration."

In a study by the National Institute on Aging, their researchers linked loneliness to a variety of physical diseases, saying, "Research has linked social isolation and loneliness to higher risks for a variety of physical and mental conditions: high blood pressure, heart disease, obesity, a weakened immune system, anxiety, depression, cognitive decline, Alzheimer's disease, and even death." Director Steve Cole, PhD of the Social Genomics Core Laboratory at the University of California, Los Angeles, explained, "Loneliness acts as a fertilizer for other diseases. The biology of loneliness can accelerate the buildup of plaque in arteries, help cancer cells grow and spread, and promote inflammation in the brain leading to Alzheimer's disease. Loneliness promotes several different types of wear-and-tear on the body."

Studies are fine and mostly good, and Dr. Cole obviously provides excellent research and information about loneliness, but as we considered this loneliness issue, we wondered if all seniors find it difficult to cope with loneliness. And how do they feel being alone day after day, night after night? After all, humans are social critters, enjoying meeting and talking to others.

While some seniors, widowed or not, seem to push aside the loneliness question, indicating they are happy with their lives and don't want to involve themselves with others, some acknowledge their loneliness and either do something about it or give in to their insecurities, fear of rejection, or unwillingness to take a chance. We can't help but think that the opposite is true: since loneliness and depression are tightly linked, could it be that laughter, change, and adventure can do the opposite and increase positive brain activity and reduce depression in older adults?

Gail wrote a blog about small towns and opened a thread of responses about loneliness:

This morning I read a Facebook post talking about loneliness, that is, the difficulty of living alone. I get that. Being alone is hard and unhealthy, according to experts smarter than I am. Being with others gives us the opportunity to laugh, argue, tease, and lament. How can I possibly argue the price of gas or lament about the cold weather or cuss out the politicians all by myself. For that matter, who wants to laugh alone? Laughter takes more than one person, and let's face it: the late-night television pundits or evening sitcoms are not as funny as Johnny Carson and Lucille Ball were.

The Cowboy and I were seated in the small central room of a local café having coffee and a forbidden sweet roll, while in the next room sat a group of about a dozen men, doing the same thing, drinking coffee and sampling the breakfast fare. You can pretty much see this scene any morning in any small town in America, people hashing over the weather and opinions about anything important in their life. The small-town culture requires that people talk to each other, get to know each other, worry about them when they don't show up for coffee and sweet rolls. They put away their cell phones and look each other squarely in the eye and talk about everything. They share. They share. They share and they aren't lonely.

As I thought about the FB post I received earlier and compared it to this happy scene, I wondered why some people are so lonely while others are bursting at the seams with friends and people they know. It seems they understand that loneliness is a paradox. If every lonely person sought out another lonely person, the ailment itself would disappear.

For his birthday one year, I bought my son a book entitled, **Stand Up, Shake Hands, Say How Do You Do.** *It's a good book for teaching kids about manners, but actually, it really is a lesson on how not to be lonely. This is a good lesson for all of us at any age. Let's get together to share a laugh face-to-face.*

Loneliness, an Invisible Disease

The comments on this blog ranged from donuts to doorbells, but one reader from Idaho, Clint B, wrote this:

Humans are overwhelmingly social animals and loneliness is soul crushing and usually self-imposed. Our own insecurities often keep us from enjoying casual companionships when, for whatever reason, we don't have a committed partner in our lives. Our insecurity centers around our inherent fear of rejection, and overcoming this requires an individual to have a different mindset. Instead of taking non-acceptance personally, we must put it in perspective. It's them, not me. Maybe they are engaged in a very personal conversation and maybe their own insecurities make them uncomfortable about interacting with strangers. One thing is certain. If a person doesn't put him- or herself out there, loneliness is almost certain to be a constant companion.

Gail wrote this blog for our Facebook audience about small towns and bumped into the loneliness issue almost by accident. Although the blog's intent recognized the popularity and usefulness of cafés in small-town America with people meeting people for a cup of coffee and a sweet roll on a regular basis, Clint saw it as a remedy for loneliness, which was not the blog's original intent. But he was right. The café provides the facility and coffee, but people's need for communication is fulfilled by the other people who show up. No one makes an appointment or asks permission; they just show up and join in the conversation, whatever it might be, family, politics, the weather, the price of gas or hay. They meet daily, weekly, monthly, talking about nothing and everything, but nevertheless talking. On this particular day, strangers and friends interacted with smiles and jokes, even teasing, about life and living in a small town. There is no dress code, and those at the tables wore seed caps, cowboy hats, or stocking caps. You can't be late or early because you arrive when you arrive. We heard discussions about studded snow tires and what brand of fertilizer is best. The local mountain lion had been sighted, and everyone cautioned each other about keeping their pets safe. Politics were mentioned, but without animosity, just shaking their heads or politely disagreeing. People came and went, but the conversation continued, and everyone was accepted, listened to, and respected.

For the widowed, conversations about their memories and their simple pleasures, such as their pets, fill the void, but conversations about life and living are important too. So many of us widowed have been cast into a sea of loneliness and deal with the sounds of silence every day, and sometimes those lonely days linger and stretch into years. But take it from us: new things, new ideas, adventures, and moving ahead will spark interest and fill the loneliness gap.

CHAPTER 4

Should I Throw Away My Knitting and Buy New Dancing Shoes?

Deciding whether to stay with the status quo or to change your life requires thinking about moving out of your comfort zone and doing something different, and, of course, offers the possibility of rejection, which can be scary. We admit that the status quo usually is comfortable, and changing directions requires decisions and a lot of work, especially when we feel that life has thrown us something that isn't the least bit fair. But remember what we drilled into our kids' thick skulls when they complained about life not being fair?

"Much of life is not fair," we reasoned. "Get over it," or in cruder terms, "Suck it up, Buttercup." The death and ensuing grief, despair, and inevitable silence after losing a spouse are also "not fair" and are significantly more difficult than our kids being grounded for a week or two. However, moving forward, recognizing and remembering the good, and leaving the bad in the rearview mirror are parts of the grieving and healing process. It is difficult and scary to change or allow change to enter your life. These changes should not be done without serious thought and consideration of the good, bad, and ugly. And while dating may seem frightening, maybe think of it differently, an opportunity for adventure, handholding, fun and games, laughter, and trips down a yellow brick road to wherever life leads. And maybe some dancing.

❧ Gail's Story ❧

I like to knit, and it eases my arthritis, so after Tom died, I once again began knitting while watching the mindless television shows. I have a great stocking cap pattern, and I bought out the dollar store's yarn supply and launched my nightly avocation, a stocking cap a day. He had been gone for nearly three hundred days, which meant three hundred colorful caps sat on my table, waiting for distribution to someone, somewhere. I didn't care where, because they helped my arthritis cure. My daughter dropped by and took a look at the caps. "What in the world are you doing?" as if she didn't know what a stocking cap looked like.

"Caps, I'm making caps. Do you want one?" I answered with a smile. "These yellow and black ones are pretty, and aren't they the colors for the University of Idaho?"

"Really, Mom? Caps? What are you going to do with them all. You are in a rut. Dad is gone, so do something to get out of your rut. You have a lot going for you—good health, you like to travel. You have done a lot of interesting things in life, so go for it. Find something you like to do." She was in her scolding mood, so I didn't reply.

She left, taking a few caps for one of her charities. Great idea, but what and who would I do it with? Traveling alone was for the birds, and I was too old to go back to school. I didn't want to get a job or volunteer because that would take a chunk out of my already busy day, so what was left? It would take some thought. Besides, what was wrong with caps?

About the same time, my friend Lucy asked if I was interested in online dating, but I shook my head. I had heard of it and considered it for forty-year-old divorcees, not seventy-five-year-old widows. I had heard all the warnings and refined the old chant to Butcher, Baker, Axe Murderer, Thief. A different friend told me she had tried online dating and met somebody. They were together now, and she seemed okay; at least she wasn't dead. As an afterthought to our discussion, she threw out a quote by writer Tucker Max: "The devil doesn't come dressed in a red cape and pointy horns. He comes as everything you've ever wished for." The devil? Oh, my gosh. Was this something I wanted to get into? I didn't know what she meant, so I told her I needed time to think this through, trying to get my head turned on straight. Was I lonely enough to face the devil or go online, where thousands or even millions of axe murderers or devils might lie in wait?

I had a hatchet, and I laughed at the thought of my using a hatchet, sure that an axe would top a hatchet any day. Still, dating was an alternative to knitting caps twelve hours a day, volunteering, returning to school, and certainly better than being alone. I could keep an eye out for the devil.

After living seven decades, and now widowed, the question was: Should I even consider online dating? The answer varies from person to person, depending on the many things that have occurred in our life—many of which cannot be changed. We all struggle deciding the right and wrong in our decisions, not only about dating, but also in every part of our life, from car buying to whether we need more than a latte for dinner. And now we must make those decisions alone. We try to decide if what we want is normal and, for that matter, healthy. We also may ask ourselves if this is all there is. Will my life always be the way it is now, or can I have more?

The answers depend on what we are willing to do and risk—yes, risk. We can remain with the status quo, our cocoon, perfectly happy, and not create any uncomfortable ripples in our life, which is certainly a choice. Living with the status quo may be the right choice, but there are alternatives that will help us decide if we should try on those dancing shoes and take to the floor, doing the jitterbug or tango or simply a Texas two-step. Shall we stay where we are, or shall we take a chance? It's up to each of us to enjoy the limited time we have in this world and make the most of it.

When life happens and our *One and Only* turns into our *Dearly Departed*, widowhood and widowerhood become a reality. Most of us have quietly thought about our spouse's death, but few of us consider how it will feel to be alone in an empty house day after day for the remainder of our lives. The emptiness and loneliness come crashing down on us when we realize there is nothing more.

As a couple ages together, they ask each other a basketful of questions, like where their youth went and how many years they have left. What is the status of their health? Do they have enough resources to continue their current lifestyle? They consider these questions for two people, not one. And then the tragedy of losing a spouse happens, and they are suddenly faced with reality. Hospice, churches, and other grief agencies work with the widowed to help them through the grieving process, but after the funeral and the friends and family have gone home, the house lies empty and silent, and the widowed must deal with a new type of life, no longer half of a couple, rather a widow, an unmarried or single person. Within a year or sometimes longer after losing their beloved, the silence begins reverberating through their brains, and some begin to yearn for something more. So, what do they do? Take a risk or maintain the status quo, like knitting another three hundred caps?

For many, the thought of going on a date never crosses their mind, and if it does, who would they date and how would they meet someone? There's a good chance they've never taken a second look at another person, remembering the "until death do us part" wedding vows. They had fallen in love and stayed in love, but now those vows had come to an end. They might have friends who are now widowed or divorced, and the idea of dating that person, someone in their circle of friends or in their church group or a former high school classmate, seems awkward.

Long-married widows and widowers have been half of a couple for much of their adult life, which could mean twenty, thirty, or fifty years of couple-hood. Their friends were couples, and they went places and entertained others as couples. Dinner for two or four was common, but now it's three, and friendly couples are reluctant to invite a single person, which brings you to a dinner for one, often something simple, possibly unhealthy, but who cares? Dining on microwave popcorn or ice-cream bars suddenly seems reasonable and desirable, and what widowed person hasn't skipped a few meals now and then, choosing instead a latte or a glass of wine or a container of yogurt and calling it good? It's easier than making a meat loaf or a chef's salad, and what difference does it make anyway? Who's to know? But for many, something is missing, the social life, the Friday night dates, and the camaraderie of mixed couples. And laughter and conversation.

Many widows and widowers search for answers. And the answer is simple. Meet someone. Say "How do you do," have a date that includes laughter and conversation, and decide whether it was better or worse than the status quo. Although the answer is simple, it begs other questions of how, who, where, and when. Perhaps that silver-haired soul at church isn't exactly the right answer, but at least they are asking the questions. One answer to the dating question of "how" is to use the Internet. Maybe this is good and right, but only after due diligence should they decide to try out this new dance move.

Women have additional fears of safety. Girls are taught to be careful, even as young as six years old, "Don't talk to strangers," but now when you online date, you are suddenly showing a photo of yourself to thousands of people, and the mere thought may scare the dickens out of you. The Internet is both an asset and a liability. When you hit send on a dating app, you don't know whether you have answered a question or invited an invisible person into your life.

Transition from Status Quo to Adventure

The "What If" syndrome happens when a basketful of doubt dumps itself in our laps. What if this? What if that? It is real and can sneak up and destroy rational thinking. What if it doesn't work out? What if my kids don't approve? What if my dead spouse's siblings accuse me of two-timing her or him? What if I get hurt or my online date steals my Social Security or retirement earnings and I end up penniless? What if I don't like dating? What if he or she jilts me, and once again I am left alone?

Questions for widows and widowers continue to plague us with a lot of what ifs, and undoubtedly one of the plagues is money. Money is important to those of us on pensions, social security, and savings, and we mostly get along with what we have, having made those decisions years ago with our now-deceased spouses. Nobody wants to go to the proverbial poorhouse, move in with our kids, or lose money or investments that we worked hard for (not to mention forgoing some luxuries, saving what we could, and planning for our retirement). We planned for two retirements and two Social Security checks, and the cost-of-living index shows us living expenses have risen, and inflation issues make it worse. Dating adds a level of complexity to this what-if situation, and each of us must balance the financial situation against our loneliness. Variables arise as economics enters the decision to date or not, such as, will I be better or worse off financially? What about pensions, property, estates? The list of questions goes on and on. They are all real questions, and only with confidence in yourself can you answer them, take control, and ditch the "What If's" in your life.

And now, another what if: What about dating? Dating can upset the apple cart and cause struggles in many ways, or it can ease the emotional issues caused by loneliness and be the answer to prayers. But for others, the status quo is a safe place. People may fear rejection or being hurt emotionally and, of course, financially. With those considerations, many decide that they love this safe place, the status quo, and this is acceptable.

If we decide dating, either online or through another method, is our cup of tea, financial matters must be approached with sensitivity. Sometimes loneliness overrides an objective mind and leads us into compromise, so at this stage private financial situations should remain just that, private. The decision to reveal information about our financial situation belongs to each person, and although revealing financial information tempts us, don't let a silver-tongued devil or, as we know them, gold diggers, convince you to open your purse or wallet. If you need help, don't hesitate to see an attorney or financial advisor for advice on your particular situation.

But Am I Too Old?

The question "What do I want to do for the rest of my life when I punch the retirement button?" seemed simple with a spouse and someone to talk to, but now, things are different. The bucket list, while now likely the size of a teacup, hasn't totally disappeared. These dreams help center us, keeping us focused on life and all its adventures. Filling up the bucket list was easy at age thirty, but those of us who live alone quickly realize that the task now has become far more difficult. We need goals, even little ones: laughing each day, calling a friend who might also be lonely, going to a new store and meeting the owner. Getting out of the house and doing something different, talking to people, laughing, checking out new things, like a new art display or the grand opening of a store. Even using an Uber! Any of these activities can be an adventure. And, most importantly, remembering Dr. Cole's advice, we must get out of our loneliness rut and move in a new direction. Adventure and laughter, the very things that keep us thinking and feeling young, are always just an effort away. We just have to look for them.

Prior to a spouse's death, no one ever says, "Oh, I think I'll date once I am alone. I think it would be cool to find someone new." Rather, it becomes a complicated decision, one taking time, energy, and forethought, but only when we are hit with loneliness does dating ever cross our minds. It involves consideration and evaluation of what's going on in our lives, economic, health, and the "k" word, Kids. They are certain to have an opinion! If after evaluating the situation, the "what if's" still outnumber "I like this idea," ask somebody you trust for help, a lawyer, accountant, a doctor. We aren't getting any healthier nor any younger, and that's the truth.

We gain energy from being active and adding fun adventures to our bucket list, which chase those dark clouds away. We also gain energy from those with whom we surround ourselves. Positive people breed optimism and make us hungry for more adventures, transferring positive energy from one person to another. Grief groups have their place, yet they can also put a damper on moving on with our life. Replacing grief groups with other groups, like church or senior centers, can be a positive alternative.

Let us offer a stereotype: At ages twenty to forty, we see unlimited horizons, viewing the future with open eyes and a bright countenance. The world is our oyster, or at least a crawdad. Later, perhaps between forty and sixty, we achieve many of our goals, our kids leave home, marry, maybe give us a grandchild or two. We are still young enough that we don't consider things that will physically, mentally, emotionally, or economically restrict us. Time starts to pass more quickly than ever before, and before we know it, we are eyeing retirement, counting the years or months until we reach our red-letter day with our plans intact for a healthy and happy rest-of-our-life. We celebrate our retirement and breathe a sigh of relief, "It's here! Finally!" Our bucket list overflows with ideas and hopes and dreams. We play golf or pickleball or travel or do whatever we spent our younger days planning to do, but unfortunately, we may have to deal with the physical and mental ailments life throws our way, which makes us realize we aren't as invincible as we once thought we were. A mild heart attack, a fall on the ski hill, a cancer scare will make us look twice at those horizons, but then, the worst happens, and our spouse dies, leaving us with an empty house and no plans, because the retirement plans that we so carefully made at age thirty were for two people, not one. Instead of those unlimited horizons and a giant-sized list of potential that we felt at age thirty, we find ourselves balancing on the edge of a cliff, hoping the wind doesn't blow us off the rim.

Humans like company, talking, visiting, laughing, touching each other, and those human needs don't disappear as we age or when our spouse dies. As a senior, it is even more important to be a part of others, but now, without a spouse, we must accept the responsibility to be proactive, because no one can do this for us. It remains our responsibility to take control of our life and look for adventure.

But Have You Seen Me?

As we age, we change. In appearance, we loathe those wrinkles and crinkles, wondering when and how they appeared, almost at the snap of a finger without our realizing it. They don't happen overnight, although it seems like they do. One day we have no signs of aging, and the next day our skin takes on the look of a rattlesnake's nest. What we forget are the forty years between the two looks in the mirror. Gail said she remembered the old song "Darling, I am growing old, silver threads among the gold," but as a young wife and mother, she never thought she would be the "darling" in the song.

We use creams lotions, dyes, Botox, and a myriad of other aging fixers, but in the end, they don't last and don't help much, possibly making us look five years younger, rather than the thirty we had hoped for. We do what the experts tell us, walk and exercise and try to eat right, but the aging process, inside and out, marches on, "one, two, one, two," and before long we look like our parents, checking our image in the mirror and saying, "What happened? Who is that old girl or guy?" We can't let these images stop us from conquering all those things left in our teacup. After all, it's our spirit, our frame of mind, our character that matter, not our exterior.

We've all known people covered with wrinkles, yet their spirit and outlook on life are the same as a thirty-year-old's. They think young, accept new people and ideas easily, and are excited to get up in the morning, looking forward to the adventures the new day might hold. They seem proud of their wrinkles and view them as proof of wisdom or energy instead of aging. The swashbuckling, never-look-back spirit comes from inside, from the brain, a direct link to how they view the world.

Believe us when we say that we know how difficult it is to keep a positive, can-do attitude, especially when there is no one around to laugh at our silly jokes, to bounce ideas off, go places with, and try new things. And when our spouse passes away, our lives change. The idea of trying something new seems impossible and hovers over us as a dark cloud.

Should I Throw Away My Knitting and Buy New Dancing Shoes?

Trying new things requires us to look at ourselves and determine if we can or can't, will or won't, have new adventures. But knowing that change is usually healthy, it's time to ask, "Am I ready to take the first step?"

Deciding to date opens the door to lots of opportunities, including finding a friend, a conversationalist, or someone with whom we are intellectually and maybe emotionally compatible. Perhaps we want to go on a pricey cruise and need someone willing to share expenses in a purely platonic arrangement. Do we want someone to take us to dinner now and then or meet someone who loves the opera or NASCAR as much as we do?

Dating is an adventure! Have fun, think about what his eyes look like when you first meet, notice her smile, remember the laughter, and enjoy those texting flirts with this intriguing new friend. This decision to date, online or the old-fashioned way, will open that door to a new life, a new love, or new freedom, and it certainly will not be boring!

CHAPTER 5

Dating: You Must Be Kidding

Making a decision about anything of importance can be tricky and requires a lot of time and energy, and certainly online dating is no exception to that rule. When we add in all the horror stories that we have heard about a friend of a friend of a friend or from Oprah or Dr. Phil, the risks are magnified. On the other hand, any adventure assumes some risk as does romance, and if we are to plunge into the dating pool, or at least stick a big toe in, testing the waters, this risk should be analyzed by each person, considering their own environment, desires, and situation.

The decision to date can be a simple yes or no. To date or not to date? The decision not to date, to do nothing, is still a decision leaving things as they are, the status quo, predictable, and mostly smooth but boring sailing. For many people, that's okay, even desirable and wonderful, and with that decision comes no risk and no change. No one attaches stigma when someone decides not to date or look for companionship. They are simply a widow or widower who chooses not to stick that big toe into the dating pool.

Everyone knows plenty of men and women, never married, divorced, or widowed, who get along just fine with no one special in their lives. It's a choice.

Losing the love of our life to many is so traumatic, though, that we can't imagine living through this another time. The effort required is too much to ponder. To some of us it may seem that this breaks a trust, those wedding vows of so long ago, and we cannot figure a way out of this moral dilemma. This is normal, and time may give us other options. Choosing to date again after losing a longtime love and partner is more than a quick decision. It takes thought and effort and then a little bit more thought.

What about those who are not content to spend their days alone, reading, watching television, or playing with their puppy? What are their options? How does a man or woman of a certain age meet someone who might want to venture into a bit of romance, travel, and adventure but still be compatible with our long-standing habits of slurping soup in front of the television or getting up three times a night to go to the bathroom or the occasional release of gas we all have?

The decision to do something, no matter what, has risk, but if we want more out of life—like adventure, new memories, or some hijinks—then a little risk taking just may be in the cards. No one wants to make a mistake, especially if it is going to injure you, cost you money, or affect your self-confidence. Yet, the decision to move forward to date might be the remedy to loneliness and may even put you on the path toward a new kind of happiness. Buy that new bikini and a set of water wings and dive in!

❧ *Gail's Story* ❧

Now, here I had arrived at a crossroads. I could do nothing and continue to live a safe, risk-free life, the status quo. Every day was predictable and filled with routine. I felt comfortable with my life, yet somewhat bored and probably stale in my thinking. And, if I wanted to continue to write books, I needed some adventures. I remembered Robert Frost's famous poem "The Road Not Taken," which ends:

*"Two roads diverged in a wood, and I—
I took the one less traveled by,
And that has made all the difference."*

For me the road less traveled has always been trying something new, taking a chance, seeing what happens. And that means taking a risk.

I had thought about online dating but didn't know much about it, and I was fearful of getting myself in some sort of trouble. At the ripe old age of seventy-six, I didn't need trouble. Everything I had heard about online dating on the television talk shows warned of the dangers, and in my discussions with friends and family, I doubted it would work for me. After all, my husband had been one in a million, and I was sure no one could be better. On the other hand, I knew it was popular and thought I should check it out. I was in the middle of writing a novel about seniors having a romantic fling and thought a chapter or two on online dating would be funny and appropriate. I could look at sites and not join, and no one would be the wiser, unless I told one of my friends, and they blabbed to the world. I knew a few couples who had met online, and they seemed okay, although younger than I am. The Meg Ryan-Tom Hanks flick, Sleepless in Seattle, *seemed like online dating, but I didn't remember any movies specifically about online dating, particularly aimed at seniors, although undoubtedly some are available. I wanted to know what I was getting into and decided to dive in. Boy, did I learn a lot.*

I Googled "online dating for seniors" and found a few generic articles about older people dating online. But immediately I faced a problem. Seniors, according to many sites, became senior citizens at age fifty, AARP style, but I own shoes older than fifty years. My kids are over fifty, and they bristle at the thought of being labeled as seniors. And wouldn't it be weird to date someone the same age as my kids? I,

Dating: You Must Be Kidding

naturally, had surpassed fifty long ago, but I continued to search for information. What did I need to know, and could I make this decision alone, all by myself?

I hit the Google search engine again and asked for information about plain old, traditional dating, you know, the way it used to be when we were younger. I met my husband at a concert. We were both with a group of friends, and we started talking, and the rest is history, as they say. But I didn't want to go to a concert because I don't much like today's music, and the days of Beatlemania are long gone. Plus, Elvis is dead. What else could I do? Google listed a few things, and realistically, I could meet people anywhere, but all relationships involve risk. As a widow, I needed to decide if the potential benefits were worth the trouble. Ah, phooey, I hit the send button. Let's see where this goes.

In my Google research, I found a list of the traditional ways of meeting people with the possibility of new friendships and dating.

- *Church*
- *Bar*
- *Senior Center*
- *Retirement Home*
- *Classes and Hobbies*
- *Work*
- *Volunteering*
- *Cruises or Other Group Adventures*
- *Shopping*
- *Friends*
- *Let's consider a bit about each.*

CHURCH: Any church group might be filled with people interested in a relationship, even better if the church offers a singles' group. A church group offers some real advantages, people who are like-minded and/or of a similar religious faith and values. And if all goes well, you might end up holding hands during Bible study or becoming part of the church choir, even if you only have a song in your heart, not in your voice. The possibilities are endless. On the other hand, dating in a closed environment like church, we determined, can lead to gossip, and disengaging from a relationship may be more difficult. We feel that dating in church may be like kissing your sister, and a failed romance tale will fly through the congregation faster than an empty offering plate, leading to no further romances. It could also require leaving that congregation. If you find yourself in this relationship, may God be with you!

BARS AND PUBS: Sometimes people spend time at a bar, pub, or local hangout to ward off loneliness, and it puts you in a position to meet a variety of interesting people, but going to a bar, too, can come with complications. In our generation and in our society, while a man going to a bar is generally considered okay, is going to a bar or pub alone seen as a good thing for a woman? However, times have changed, and a woman alone in a bar is not that unusual; the old stigma is out of date. If this is your comfort zone, go for it!

A tasty glass of wine is a good thing, but a steady diet—a parade of gin and tonic or whiskey and sour or rum and Coke—might not be the safest method of meeting a suitable partner or building a healthy relationship. Bars and restaurants have no filter for whom they serve; thus the customer never knows about the person who joins you for a drink. Whether you choose a good person over a not-so-good person is up to you, and alcohol may impede your judgment. You are on your own. You should consider other options, like going to places that are more geared to senior interests like the golf course club house, the pickleball gathering spot, or the local VFW or American Legion dances on Friday nights. Many of us are not aware of or forget about these choices, but ask around, and maybe you will find something safe and fun for you.

Dating: You Must Be Kidding

SENIOR CENTERS: America has a wonderful system of senior centers with hot food and entertainment from bingo to banjos, and they are certainly worthy of taking a look. The facilities are squeaky clean, and the meals are cheap or free. The people who are there are seniors, often living alone, widowed or divorced. The staff is friendly and pays attention to who attends and who is missing and may follow up when a "regular" doesn't show for a day or two. All in all, senior centers are a good thing.

Transportation is readily available, and anyone looking purely for companionship, a few hands of bridge or gin rummy, a change in routine, or a cheap and tasty, hot meal, can look toward the senior centers to see what's available. Bingo and card games are popular as well as outings to local attractions, plays, ball games, shopping trips, and sightseeing. You won't be disappointed.

Looking for love? You might find some of that too!

RETIREMENT HOMES: Retirement homes are another option, although they take a commitment of moving from one place to another. They are available in most communities, sometimes at reduced costs. You can find anything meeting your needs, such as the Villages in central Florida, where nearly 160,000 retired folks play golf on the thirty golf courses. They offer other active and passive activities, such as trips, shopping, eating out, libraries, and you can meet many new friends in similar situations. Local retirement homes, sometimes step-down facilities catering to people with close family or community ties, offer health and mental health care, and you can move from one level of care to the next without too much interruption to your daily life. Each of these options offers people to talk to, go to lunch or shopping with. The downside is having to move, and they can be expensive. You may lose some elements of privacy, and not every retirement home is perfect. If you decide to go this route, check reviews, check out their activity schedule for a couple of months prior, have more than one meal at the dining hall, and give it a good look to be sure it's right for you. It wouldn't hurt to visit several times, at various times of the day or evening, either.

As with most dating options for people our age, women outnumber men three to one. If one believes the sensationalism of various news media, some of these larger places can be rife with STDs, meaning some romance is blooming. Of course, these are all written by twenty-somethings who don't think Grandma or Grandpa should be holding hands with a stranger, and PDA among seniors is repulsive to those younger researchers. The truth is that a retirement home can be a great place to meet, greet, love, and maybe more.

CLASSES: How about a class in photography or ballroom dancing? Enrollment in skills classes attracts a variety of people. Local colleges and senior centers specialize in helping people find their niche for something they have put off for too many years. Watercolors, woodworking, yoga, travel opportunities, and more are available. These classes keep your body and brain active, and you are sure to meet new people. Some communities offer college classes at reduced rates, and you can complete your dream of getting a degree, competing with kids who are the same age as your grandkids.

We can't see a downside, except perhaps the expense involved. You'll have fun and meet new people, but remember, these classes are open to all ages, and it is possible that our age group is not always well represented. However, if you do meet someone here, you will have a lot in common intellectually, and chances are, he or she will be interested in new things.

WORK: We retire to stop working, but some of us find we miss the productive and social parts of the job, and after a period of idleness, we search for a new and different opportunity. These days many stores have "Help Wanted" signs on the front door, and some pay well too, with flexible hours and benefits. But do you want a job or to find a friend, someone to spend time with? As a reminder, dating coworkers may be frowned on by Human Resources, and you may not last long after making a pass at that lovely silver-haired coworker.

VOLUNTEERING: Every non-profit and some for-profits look for volunteers, and we applaud those who spend time and energy helping others. Volunteering is a healthy activity, improving your self-esteem and adding energy to your countenance. And maybe you will find opportunities to meet people, but remember, you are there to promote and enhance the agency. Breaking away from a volunteer agency can be difficult too. The same cautions apply about office romances. Times have changed, dating a coworker carries stigma, and the jokes you told thirty years ago will get you fired and sued today.

CRUISES OR OTHER GROUP ADVENTURES: Cruises provide miniature dating opportunities, and what a great way to meet new people from all over the world. You sit at dinner across from a small group of people you have never met before and ask them questions, learning about their past, present, and future, and hope they are truthful. You follow dinner with a drink at one of the many watering holes and maybe dance a bit. Maybe you go with them to a late-night concert or show and take a midnight stroll around the deck and return to your cabin alone or together. No strings have been knotted. If you didn't enjoy this person, sit at a different table for tomorrow's breakfast and start over again. It's a beautiful, fun way to meet people, and lots of long-term relationships have started with a moonlight walk around the deck of a ship. However, if that relationship hits the rocks, you may be trapped for the rest of the trip.

The drawback is cruises are pricey and have no filter as to whether the hot babe or silver fox is who they say they are.

SHOPPING: Who hasn't struck up a conversation with the food-taster person at Costco or spent time near the Cabela's animal display and made funny comments to another person about the grizzly swiping the salmon? Shopping is a great way to meet people, but it is a little difficult to determine marital status, so as you are chatting up this silver-haired lovely and suddenly the wife/husband appears, you had better be quick on your feet and be aware that security people rove the aisles. You don't need that kind of problem. The Costco food woman might turn you in to management and have you banned as a voyeur from the store, or the Cabela's lone person is alone because he is waiting for his wife, or she is there to buy a gun for misdeeds. Time wasted.

FRIENDS: Pre-computers, friends introduced two people through blind dates, double dates, or group dates. In the old days, it was the most popular way to meet another person and has somewhat of a filter. It was sort of an informal matchmaking opportunity, successful sometimes, but we can all remember blind date disasters. You would go on a double date with friends, have a frolicking good time, and history was in the making.

We don't really see a downside, unless things go awry, and you disappoint the matchmakers and lose a friendship because of their misguided enthusiasm.

❧ *Robert's Story* ❧

I started thinking about meeting women, wondering how I could start a conversation. I watched them at the grocery and in the beer queue line at the rodeo and everywhere else I went. I was puzzled, but at least I was thinking. Somewhere I read that a journey starts with the first step. I didn't want to scare them off but was unsure of how to take that first step, maybe a word, a smile, or a wink. What the heck?

Over the next few weeks, my life started to pick up. I lost some weight, bought some new clothes, and like a matador, I started girding up for the contest. Maybe this dating idea would help erase all that silence.

Dating: You Must Be Kidding

Just the thought of it caused my dreams to take off in directions I had not thought about in years. Patty wasn't going to come back, I knew that, but what about a different lovely woman? Hmmm, it sounded good, an improvement over self-pity.

Yahoo! A new adventure was about to begin. Who knows?

This was a whole new experience. It had been nearly fifty years since I flirted with a woman other than Patty. My first effort at talking to a lady at Costco felt weird, like I needed a script, and the lady pulled back from me as if I were a stalker. I realized I wasn't really paying attention to her sales pitch. She was demonstrating pizza bites, and her eyes grew big as I asked where she found that package of pecans. They kinda look the same, but I saw her confusion. Wow, this was hard.

I belong to a church with lady members who are approximately my age, but I could not shake the feeling that flirting was somehow like kissing my sister. I don't even have a sister and shied away from them. They still remembered Patty, and maybe it was too soon, and I decided that this was not a good plan for me. Chasing widowed women in church seemed somehow sacrilegious and would not bode well for the idea of a date.

Occasionally I go to the local bar and grill in town for a great burger and to watch the TVs mounted on the wall, but night after night looking at these denim-clad females, mostly younger than I, accompanied by coworkers or friends, seemed to suggest that the chance of meeting a classy lady in her seventies was highly unlikely. The classy lady I was searching for was probably at the opera or symphony, not at the bar. There was no whiff of perfume, mostly agrarian smells, like fresh-cut hay or the honest sweat of a long day's work. While honorable, it wasn't what I was looking for.

After a while, I talked to some of my friends, asking if they could "set me up" with someone, but that drew a blank stare, and they started talking about cows. I love talking about cows, but it wasn't the subject I *wanted to focus on. I even talked to my brother in Texas about meeting someone at his yacht club. My sister-in-law rolled her eyes, saying, "Not your type, Cowboy," and she was probably right. Those ladies wore $500 deck shoes, Rolex watches, and gold nautical earrings and would probably freeze their buns off up here in the mountains of Montana. They probably didn't even own a single pair of pacs (snow boots) or Carhartts.*

The words of my grandson came back to me about Internet dating. "It's easy. You have a computer and know how to use it. Go for it!" I fired up the laptop and Googled "Internet dating for seniors" and opened the door to a new lifestyle I had no idea existed.

Everyone is different, and there is no one-size-fits-all for meeting new people and forming new relationships. However, for everyone, it is up to you to take the first step.

CHAPTER 6

DATING: THE DEMOGRAPHICS OF SENIOR DATING

We baby boomers keep on booming. The U.S. Census Bureau predicts that in 2050, the over age sixty-five population will reach a whopping 88 million, more than double the number in 2010, growing by over 3 percent annually. If half of those were men and half were women, it would make a big splash in the dating pool; however, they also reported, "Widows accounted for 30% of all older women in 2020.

> PEW RESEARCH REPORTED THAT 13 PERCENT OF PEOPLE AGED SIXTY-FIVE OR OLDER HAVE FOUND LOVE ONLINE.

There were more than three times as many widows (8.8 million) as widowers (2.6 million)." Talk about lopsided.

Statistically, men die at a younger age than women, and stereotypically older men like to marry younger women, adding to the lopsidedness. Add to that, widowed men are more eager to marry than widowed women.

While we seniors sometimes wonder if diving into the dating pool is worth the effort, if you are willing to get your feet wet with digital dating, you can join the 300,000 or more new digital daters every month. It might be worth grabbing a towel and jumping in.

So, now we find ourselves at the most popular way to date: online dating. These sites have grown exponentially, now numbering eight thousand sites worldwide. They have improved their methods of filtering to address the risks and have added safety precautions. To fully use this dating process takes time, patience, skill, and of course, caution. It isn't for the faint of heart and takes a little bravery, but what worthwhile activity isn't fraught with risks?

According to the statistics below, online dating is currently the most popular form of dating in North America. It has outpaced all the traditional forms of dating and is now the fastest growing dating segment in the Internet dating world. As seniors, we are a unique niche, with several excellent sites catering to our needs. As we widows and widowers move forward, seeking adventure, choosing to live more bravely and beautifully, online dating is an obvious and popular choice.

Wikipedia documented its information with this chart about heterosexual couples meeting from 2009 to 2017.

Dating: The Demographics of Senior Dating

HOW HETEROSEXUAL COUPLES HAVE MET, DATA FROM 2009 AND 2017

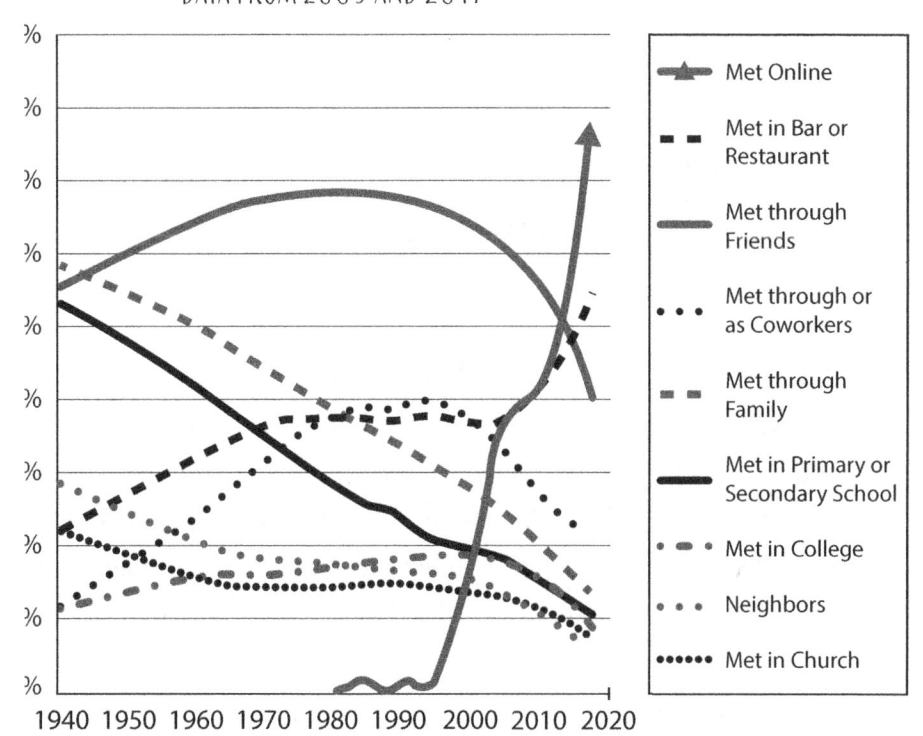

Legend:
- Met Online
- Met in Bar or Restaurant
- Met through Friends
- Met through or as Coworkers
- Met through Family
- Met in Primary or Secondary School
- Met in College
- Neighbors
- Met in Church

X-axis: 1940 1950 1960 1970 1980 1990 2000 2010 2020

Figure 1: The continued rise of meeting online for heterosexual couples.

Source: How Couples Meet and Stay Together Surveys, 2009 and 2017 waves. Consistent with Rosenfeld and Thomas (2012), all trends are from unweighted Lowess regression with bandwidth 0.8 (Cleveland 1979), except for meeting online, which is a 5 year moving average because meeting online takes place in the more recent data-rich part of the data. N=2,473 for HCMST 2009 and N=2,997 for HCMST 2017. Friends, family, and co-workers can belong to either respondent or partner. Percentages do not add to 100% because the categories are not mutually exclusive; more than one category can apply.

CHAPTER 7

Hey, Good-Lookin'!

When we crossed that dance floor, as we did at our high school sock hop days, it was "Hey, good-lookin', let's do the twist!" and good times rolled. Why did we ask that particular cutie to dance? And why was the answer YES or maybe NO? For thousands of years, we have selected mates based on what we consider important, like beauty, strength, color of eyes, or some other undefined qualities. Now, at our age, our selection criteria are way more defined. Some of our criteria are based on our past love and life companion. Did we like what we had? Do we want something different? Maybe it is somewhere in between these two.

By living our long, loving life, we know what we like and don't like. In our experience and the experience of friends and acquaintances who surround us, a couple of things stand out, divorced or widowed status being one.

Divorced, widowed, or never married is one of those filters to consider when we are searching for a companion, whether for conversation or for a long-term relationship. Is dating different for the widowed versus the divorced? We believe so. Having lost someone to death, widows and widowers have unique experiences from those who have divorced or never married. All people will view relationships and marriage through the eyes of their previous marriages and bring expectations from that marriage to a new relationship. They will compare it with what they had, what they think they want, and may tread lightly to form a new relationship. If widows and widowers had a long, happy marriage, they may expect future relationships to have the same positive outcomes and work hard to make it happen. They know what it takes to have a good, successful marriage.

Similarly, the divorced view life and love through the eyes of their failed marriage, regardless of whose fault it was, and skepticism follows them around, sometimes making them reluctant to fully accept the new person. A divorce is the result of voluntary choices made by one or both partners. A divorced person has certainly experienced loss and tragedy, but the spouse remains alive, possibly in the picture, and probably available for conversation and support even when the split wasn't amicable.

A divorced person may not have experienced the tragic, catastrophic, or sometimes unexpected loss of a spouse, making it difficult to understand the pain and emotional costs of caregiving that many widowed persons have experienced. The long-term marriage, caregiving for a sick or disabled spouse, and finally the loss experience will profoundly influence the widowed in their view of relationships. Sometimes people die suddenly, other times bit by bit, but in either case, the surviving spouse remains behind to pick up the pieces, including the remaining family issues that sometimes can last for years.

Losing someone you love is traumatic, so it's understandable that some may not want to be hurt again or repeat the taxing experience of being a caregiver. They are reluctant to spend another chunk of time and money or energy taking care of an invalid spouse. Widows and widowers who are contemplating finding a new partner are often vigilant about deciding to link up with a new person and may adhere to an often-heard phrase: "I wouldn't mind having someone else in my life, but I don't want to be a nurse or a purse or even worse."

Those who have spent years as a caregiver, or even those who haven't, may be cautious about diving into the role of spouse again for many reasons that are stated above and most certainly include financial ramifications. If you have ample income, will a new person drain your resources? If your income level allows you to barely squeak by, will you be better or worse off connecting with another person? And if you are happy with your life as it is, how will things change, making your life better or worse, dragging you into places you do not intend to go, or soaring into a new life and new experiences? And what about your children and other family members? They are sure to have an opinion! These are more valid questions that deserve review before starting to date.

But for those of us who want more out of life, remember that all of this is a bunch of hooey, because the touch of her hand or his wink and smile when he sees you will dissolve all these left-brained concerns, and you'll know the blue-eyed cowboy or silver-haired lovely is the adventure you are looking for.

Of course, widowed and divorced persons get together all the time, so a general statement about widows matching up with widowers simplifies the issue, and each relationship stands on its own strength. Romance and love are strong emotions and bind together diverse people with matches that are indescribable, lovely, and beautiful. Romance becomes the adventure of moving from loneliness and proverbial darkness to the technicolor of life.

More Considerations

Spirit comes to mind as we consider other areas of importance in looking for a common soul. The word "spirit" is nearly impossible to define, yet when someone has spirit, you know it. A spirit of adventure can be manifested in a wide range of interests ranging from politics,

Hey, Good-Lookin'!

religion, environment, family, or going to bingo at the local VFW hall every Friday night. You know what you like in life, or at least you are pretty sure you know. This is your chance to choose someone who is compatible with your sense of adventure. This adventure may be such a thing as staying home with hot cocoa with your fur baby curled up on your feet or climbing Mt. Everest and is different for everyone. As you make online choices, decide the importance of this spirit as it relates to you. For instance, Gail is a traveler. Robert is too. Being with someone who does not share the same spirit would smother or ignore the other.

To be sure, all relationships require compromises, but at this stage of the dance, go for the gusto. It is too difficult at our age to change someone, and heaven help us, we don't want anyone to change us. Online dating offers a multitude of options. Look at the photos, read the profiles, send a wink or a smile to the ones who seem intriguing, and let the music start.

For those who have read this far, you can see clearly that Internet dating for seniors is the new nirvana. The demographics show thousands of potential silver-haired Romeos or Juliets waiting for your post, your profile, and a photo that fits their idea of the perfect choice for a relationship, whether it be intellectual, emotional, or that romp in the hay. Take that first step to romance and adventure. And hit "SEND."

CHAPTER 8

Taking It Slow and Easy

These first steps in the online dating process are fun and should lead to meeting someone, so, it is time to ask, "What's next?" What do you want? Do you want short term or, as the kids say, "a hookup," or long term, which can mean many things. We, Robert and Gail, agreed that a long-term relationship, built on honesty and compatibility, is what each of us was after. So, we decided to break down some steps of this dating adventure that led to our success. Think of these steps as an outline for the adventure, not a detailed plan, but what comes next in a linear progression. (Gail does not believe in linear, so she wants to immediately "get to it" and not think about it. "After all," she says, "this is romance, not building a darn airplane." Therefore, there is no checklist, but this is a "fuzzy" list of steps.)

❧ *Gail's Story* ❧

I spent a few more weeks wrestling through the idea of dating, online or traditional, trying to decide if either would work for me. I looked at myself in the mirror and frowned. Does online dating mean more than a gentle conversation, like sleeping with someone, you know, having sex? At my age? Why would I even want to have sex, and who would want to have sex with me, a dried-up, wrinkly prune? Menopause lay

Taking It Slow and Easy

in the rearview mirror, thank heavens, although my hot flashes were still raging. And did I really want to date? What would we talk about? I used to have a lot of female friends to go to lunch with, but they were mostly silent now too. I was comfortable with myself, I had the library with lots of books I hadn't read, I was in the middle of writing at least one new book, and I didn't really need someone to talk to, although the echoing emptiness had begun to bother me. It sounds like an oxymoron, but the longer I listened, the louder the sounds of silence grew, and soon my daughter's voice repeated her warning in my brain, "Get out of your rut." I wondered how to get the booming silence out of my ears.

I remembered while doing my online research for a book that an ad had popped up and begun flashing, "Online Dating for People Over Seventy, Click Here." I had thought about this a few times, but maybe the time was now. I looked around and verified no one, including the devil, had sneaked into my house, relieved I was home alone. Who would know? How hard could it be? I searched out the site and hit the "Click Here" button to check out the advertisement, and in seconds a bunch of gray-headed men appeared on my screen, all with their shirts open, displaying white chest hair three buttons down. My late husband never wore his shirts loose at the neck because he wore polos, often stained or frayed, but I didn't care because it meant we were together, alive, and doing something.

I must admit the men in the advertisement looked handsome, some with cool haircuts, engaging eyes, tanned, and physically fit. They entranced me because none of the men at church, the senior center, or Costco resembled their style. None of the men and women in the promo photos had bald heads or saggy skin. Models, I thought. Or mannequins. Too good to be true. I clicked off and returned to my research.

After a somewhat sleepless night where my dreams had a bit of sauciness, first thing the next morning, I had an epiphany and thought I would take a second look at this online dating thing. I went on a single, free site and filled in the blanks and sent a snapshot. I had six people contact me within four minutes. Larry and Joe sent smiles. Fisherguy sent a thumbs-up, Mike sent a heart and told me what a great smile I had, and New Guy had no picture and said, "Hi," and I wondered whether he was a real person or computer generated. Richard texted, "Are you, by chance, a Russian?" which I thought weird. I looked at the pictures for a few minutes and called a friend who had more experience with online dating, because it was obvious that I didn't know what I was doing. She didn't help me much, but we threw out Richard and New Guy. All six matches were between seventy and eighty and looked pretty good, although Fisherguy's and Larry's photos were a little blurry, apparently selfies. New Guy hadn't answered most of the questions, which was reason enough to exclude him from my online dating experience. I'm not Russian, so I swiped left to get rid of Richard. Would one of these Romeos take the next step? I sent a "heart" to Joe and Mike and a "thumbs-up" to Larry and Fisherguy and did an interior shrug. Was I getting ahead of myself?

❧ Robert's Story ❧

I like to investigate things before I jump, so as I contemplated online dating, I Googled "Internet dating for seniors" and looked over all the highlights, unsure of what to look for. Promises and endorsements appeared on all sites and sounded wonderful, but all of them sounded the same. Over the next couple of days, with little to go on, I kept reading about dating sites, some for seniors and even a few for cowboys. I narrowed my sites down to three, fitting my age and interest. As I opened these sites, I was asked for pictures and a profile and filled out the minimum information and clicked the send button, thinking that this *is a lot like sending in box tops for that Gene Autry six-gun sixty years ago and wondering if I was about to get the same results.*

The next morning when I fired up the computer, I saw messages, from women, winking, waving, and sending me smiles. I, the kid in high school who couldn't get a date, was being flirted with by several good-looking vixens. I sat back in my chair and remarked to Cody, my faithful dog, "Good grief, this is amazing." Then I looked at each of the ladies, reviewed their profiles, and decided I would answer some of them with a corresponding wink or smile. Two were on the West Coast, Oregon and California, a little far from Montana, but I decided to give it a shot and returned icons to all of them. I then started writing a text message, asking if they liked Paris. I love Paris. Paris is for lovers, and romance is what I was looking for. Well, one answered, and we started talking about art, which grew to other subjects. Then some others answered, and I kept looking, which was a great start to this Internet thing. It was a fun start to the day.

One was from Texas and told me she had already started packing her suitcase to move to Montana, but that was a little fast for this old cowboy, so I politely demurred and moved on. Another started telling me about her deceased husband's demise, and although I sympathized, I closed her out too. My lonely hours disappeared, lost in a haze of text messages to lovely widow women that began to consume every evening hour. I was on my computer nightly from 6:30 to 7:30 with Ginger, from 8:00 to 9:00 with Jo, and 9:00 to 11:00 with Winter; she was a texter! Then one said, "Let's meet halfway between my place and yours for a cup of coffee." Wahoo, this was great! You could not have wiped the smile off my face with a bucket of cold water. The adventure was on!

Building a relationship takes time, often years, and entails a lot of work as we try to keep a steady foot passing over those inevitable bumps in the road. Relationships are a form of intimacy, drawing two people together as friends. Usually, successful couple relationships pass through three stages, which we call: **intellectual intimacy, emotional intimacy, and physical intimacy**. They build on each other and generally pass in order. Physical intimacy without the other two will be strained, what some might call "one-night stands."

Intellectual intimacy means getting to know someone, talking, laughing, texting, flirting, and generally spending time together, either electronically, by phone, or in person. The aim of a texting conversation and early phone calls is to gain a sense of who the other person is. Am I comfortable with how they express themselves? How will my friends and family respond to them? While a new companion will not replace our former spouse, we want to feel at ease when introducing him or her to our family and circle of friends. If they are also widowed, have they dealt with the loss of their spouse, and are they ready for a new person in their life, or do they have feelings of betraying their former spouse, uncertain of whether to move forward? Are they able to see how a new person fits into their life, or will grief still hover around them? And the basic, most important question is do you like him or her?

At this intellectual level, we are not quite ready to give our hearts away. The platonic conversations will be about family, past adventures, careers, dreams, and goals. Questions, laughter, and good, strong conversation will help build further levels of communication. These conversations give each person a feel for the intellectual capacity and cultural background of the other person. Are you compatible? Do you jive with each other? Do you laugh?

For those of us who are widowed, a text or phone call will most likely consist of conversation and trying people on, checking to see if we like them. Does he or she fit like an old sweater or rub like an ill-fitting shoe? It is difficult to step inside the other person's brain to know his or her intention, so the goals of simply having an interesting conversation and some smiles and laughs are good ones. But do both people have the same goal? What things do I have in common with my match/date? Can I talk to him or her or am I met with dead silence because the other person has nothing to say, or I have nothing to say back?

At this stage, we may be texting multiple people, but texting more than three people simultaneously can overload a brain and texting skills. It is so easy to mix up Sally, the teacher, with Sandra, the bookkeeper, or John, the farmer, with Joe, who collects exotic plants. They may live in four different states and be interested in different things, which can be confusing. Sometimes these texting sessions work out and the relationship grows, but other times they dead end.

FDA: The first goal of online dating is to have a First Date Adventure, what we call an FDA. An FDA will be built on the conversations and compatibility found with this person during texting and/or phone calls. The normal sequence is to text within the dating app. At this point, your identity remains hidden; only your name and whatever information you share with your profile will be seen by your person of interest, who is on the other end of the text.

The next normal step after gaining a sense of trust, including asking about axes, is to share your personal text contact information, usually your phone number. This step is usually initiated by one partner and agreed to by the other and comes after several in-app texting sessions. Caution: This step will reveal personal contact information. Make sure you are ready.

Texting with your own personal phone number, of course, perhaps leads to a phone call, and this important step allows you to listen to your "paramour's" voice, how they speak. It is another opportunity to learn about this person. For you really brave people, FaceTime can be accessed, and now, wahoo, you'll see if this lovely person even resembles the photo you have perused all these days.

If all goes well—you like the voice, the conversations, and you have a sense of comfort as much as is possible over a phone conversation—this is the time to go for it. "We need to meet." Someone will say those words, and it will be time to accept or reject the FDA.

Emotional intimacy moves us into stage two, connecting with someone, meaning getting to know each other. This stage usually comes after the FDA. It may come on fast or perhaps little by little and includes developing some feelings about the other person and having those emotions returned. A sense of liking and maybe loving occurs at this stage. We feel an emotional connection, and the idea of commitment bounces in and out of our hearts and brains, although neither may voice their feelings. And more questions emerge. Are your conversations filled with excitement, interrupting because you are so eager to answer? Do you like the way they sound? Are you comfortable with how they look? Are they clean and neat to your satisfaction? Do they have acceptable manners in conversation and interaction? Do they smile a lot? Do they make you laugh? Are they prompt with their phone dates? Are they willing to mention their kids and deceased spouse respectfully and without sadness? You may have feelings for this person, anticipating conversations and yearning for more.

Emotional intimacy builds on intellectual intimacy and usually is started by the things we have learned and experienced by texting or phoning—all of which may lead to the FDA. The FDA is a milestone in the relationship. It takes you out of the Internet world and drops you into the world of reality, IRL, in real life. The FDA allows all the senses to survey and experience the other person. You see them, smell them, hear them, see how they walk and talk and carry on a conversation. You will be able to notice if they have any mannerisms that are taboo. For example, do they avoid looking in your eyes when they talk to you or use a lot of "uhs" and "ers"? Do they not answer questions about themselves? Is laughter a part of their personality, or do they prefer solemnity? You hear them laugh, notice their smile, and you determine for yourself if they are truly interested in you and your story. Emotional intimacy requires that you be yourself, not who you would like to be, a real person with ideas and opinions, hopes and dreams, and the ability to laugh at yourself.

Emotional intimacy can also be called the romance stage. Some consider romance old-fashioned, but it isn't. Rather it is the backbone of all emotional relationships, from a bouquet of flowers to a kiss on the cheek to handholding and more. Romance shows someone you like them, without commitment, just because you like them. It can be more than good manners or a smile at the right time. Opening the car door or helping them on with their coat or making a pot of tea or coffee. Listening. Laughing at the same joke. Romance is found in the oddest places, but it is critical at this stage of a budding relationship.

Emotional intimacy marks a time of giving information, but how much is the right amount? Certainly, family details, kids, ages, brothers, sisters, and parents are fair subjects. Maybe discuss travel history, travel plans, and bucket list? What about our hopes and dreams as well as frustrations. Or work history or community involvement. But we need to tell the truth, *no lies*, regardless of the fib level. For example, if a match says he or she is a scratch golfer and you say "Me too," what happens when you are invited to the driving range and you say, "What kind of cars?" Now, this may seem like an exaggeration, but it's the little lies that can trip you up. And, as we noted earlier, but certainly worth repeating, the definite no-no: financial information, regardless of whether you are financially well off or wondering how you will pay the rent. It's off limits. If financial issues arise during texting or phone calls, remind him or her simply and plainly, "Discussions about money are off limits, at least for the time being." He or she will respect you for your frankness, but if not, you probably haven't lost anything, including your life's savings.

Emotional intimacy also takes us to a higher level of intimacy or commitment, such as a one-on-one relationship. For widows and widowers, making room in our heart for a second person is a serious leap of faith, moving from the past to the present and acceptance of having a permanent link to someone new for communication or connection. Giving your heart to another person does not mean that you didn't love the other with all your heart. It simply means that your emotions are transitioning to a new love.

Talking to and enjoying a person is one thing, but committing to him or her is a whole different can of applesauce. After a marriage ending with years of pain and suffering, or maybe a quick and sudden death, we understand the marriage relationship and the necessary commitment involved, meaning the commitment discussion is no stranger to the widowed. And it is up to the individual to understand when and how to talk about commitment, not too pushy, but not too passive. Your common sense and experience will guide you.

The third stage, **physical intimacy**, can be scary for some, giving even the most confident of daters second thoughts because it might require a further level of commitment—sex. Physical intimacy, though, encompasses many forms: touching, hugging, and perhaps swapping spit. It means much more than just slipping between the sheets. It is a touch of a hand, a kiss, the lingering touch on a cheek, a quick or not-so-quick hug, and a long goodbye with hands slowly pulling apart. These sexual longings are not leftover relics from our teenage hormonal rages, but a natural extension of intellectual and emotional intimacy.

In our high school days, stern principals frowned on PDA (public display of affection) as they stood in the middle of the hall grimacing and pointing, calling out, "Hey, you two, cool it." Thank goodness we have

Taking It Slow and Easy

outgrown the PDA stigma and now, in our advanced age and wisdom, can relish holding hands, hugging, and kissing in public. Even stealing a kiss in a crowded movie theater or restaurant rings our bells. When we seniors steal that kiss or smile longingly into the other's eyes, it brings smiles and sometimes applause from an impromptu audience. Sometimes, we have found, the impromptu, innocent pecks are accompanied by "Woot! Woot! Aren't they cute?"

The level of physical intimacy indicates commitment. Both are willing to give themselves to the other, mentally, emotionally, and now physically. It may or may not include marital commitment, because the world has changed, and let's face it, we have changed. When we silver-haired oldies were just little frogs, physical intimacy had lots of worries and strings attached: pregnancy, a marriage license, and chastisement from our family and friends. But that isn't the case for us seniors. Pregnancy would be a colossal surprise and evoke a whole host of scientific studies. And we probably aren't competing for a record for number of marriages, like Frank Sinatra or Elizabeth Taylor. Societal rules have abated, even changed, and having a physical relationship with another person who is about our age doesn't have the stigma it did a hundred, or fifty, or even twenty years ago. We live longer and are healthier, and we often hear that sixty is the new forty or eighty is the new sixty. Caution: Watch out for STDs!

Boundaries should be discussed, because saying "No" to any phase of intimacy is an option, but saying "Yes" is also an option. Conversations about these choices should be open, honest, and without embarrassment. Physical intimacy is a big step particularly for a widow or widower who lived with one partner for many years. We are older, our bodies are probably not centerfold material, so privacy and modesty concerns should be observed with love and care. Long, lingering pillow talks are a nice way to end the day and start the night with a bed-scape of romance.

Loving Again

Gail recently asked her friend Steve, who had been widowed several years ago and seemed desperate for conversation, if he had ever thought about online dating. His answer, "Not really, because I'm not ready to hop into bed with someone I don't know. I had a satisfying relationship with Marianne and don't want to sleep with someone else. I'd feel like a traitor, betraying my wedding vows."

Gail commented, "I know you loved Marianne with all your heart, but how about having a meaningful conversation with someone, learning about them, you know, new people, new thoughts. You don't have to sleep with someone to have a conversation with them."

Steve's comment is common among people our age who, for whatever reasons, may fear rejection or being hurt emotionally, and decide that they do not want any form of intimacy. They rationalize ways to thwart anything that might lead to a long-term relationship. Premarital sex and other taboos are often woven into our psyche and may serve as a part of this rationalization. The status quo for many seniors is a safe place, the only safe place.

Our hearts and minds will always carry a level of passion for our deceased spouses, but when we begin to date, we must make room in our hearts and minds for new adventures, not comparing one to the other. And with our new adventures, we should open our minds as widely as possible with the understanding we are making this choice to live life fully and beautifully.

Deciding on a new direction takes courage, even stamina, but we will never know the beauty until we try. These steps all take work, time, and commitment and should give you a good idea of building a relationship after you have sent that first wink, thumbs-up, or smile.

CHAPTER 9

But Wait! What Is Grandma Up to Now?

But wait! Other considerations are certain to arise for the senior provocateur as they dive into online dating, and one of these is "What the heck is Grandma up to?" spoken by adult children, grandchildren, and siblings of the deceased.

Our family and close friends provide a tapestry that wraps around us and brings us comfort. It binds us to our loved ones, and most people retain the tapestry throughout their lives, adding relatives, friends, in-laws, and out-laws into the fold. Prior to the age of electronics, family members and good friends would come and go, and we sometimes lost track of them as they moved, married, divorced, or changed jobs. But now the Internet and social media have created ways to retain and renew those whom we lost through the years. When someone dies, oftentimes the family is reunited, and the tapestry fully bounces back to life, but it may also strengthen or weaken with feelings of loss, grief, and guilt. Some families come together, and others drift apart, but a death changes the tapestry as well as the roles of the widowed. Adult children and grandchildren no longer have one of their parents or grandparents, which causes a shift in family dynamics. These changes are complex and take time to evolve. Those adult children may feel the need to assume more responsibility, or they may back away from intruding in the life of the surviving spouse.

In addition, familial roles change with time. As we age, our needs change, and as our children mature, they will see life through different lenses. Parents are parents and children are children, but with a death, parents and their adult children may swap their roles. If and when that happens, parents become their children, and the adult children become their parents, especially when mental or physical health becomes an issue. Adult children may restrict their parents from driving, monitor their money, force them to move into different housing, limit travel and spending, and attend medical and legal appointments with them. Sometimes children put curfews on their parents and even do their grocery shopping. These restrictions may be needed, other times not.

❧ Gail's Story ❧

My family tapestry changed when Tom died. Although I had been the family decision maker throughout the years, only Tom and I knew it. However, he was not one to stand on the outside of the circle, and our family looked to him for strength and wisdom. When he became ill, my role strengthened, but he was still perceived as the go-to person, so my children and other family members seemed surprised when I asserted myself to what they thought was his role.

I felt comfortable with my new role, although it really wasn't new. On the other hand, I didn't have anyone to bounce questions and ideas off, and occasionally, I made the mistake of going to my children for advice, such as a major purchase, GE, LG, or Bosch dishwasher, or whether I should move to Spain or France, or enroll in pilot's school, or learn to sky dive. Or, worst of all, what was their opinion about voting for one person or another. Perhaps they interpreted my asking their advice in

But Wait! What Is Grandma Up to Now?

these limited occasions as my wanting them to become my parent. That was a no-brainer, and I would never let that happen.

When I lost my husband, my children lost their father, and their kids lost a grandpa. He had been a good father and loved them deeply, paying attention to what they did and who they did it with, teaching them sports, guiding them in their decision making about careers and college, and teaching them silly songs.

My friends reacted differently too. A few weeks after Tom died, I was on the receiving end of a couple of conversations like this: "Hey, Gail, are you looking to date someone? If so, you should check out old Mort down the street. He's lost two wives but is looking for someone else. You'd get along fine with him. Although eighty, he's a young eighty, and mostly healthy. He likes to eat and you're a good cook, so why don't you check him out?"

Hmm, *I thought,* he wants a cook, and what does "mostly healthy" mean? *Which part wasn't healthy? Heart, prostate, liver, kidney? Was he looking for a friend, companion, caregiver, or wife? In that conversation I saw myself in an apron, cooking and cleaning, and I am sorry to say,* "Been there, done that." It took barely a minute for this Marine to inform my friend that poor old Mort would have to get along without me. When I dismissed them, my matchmaker friends and relatives interpreted my rejecting Mort as rejecting anyone and assumed I would continue to live as I had, traveling alone or with one of my female relatives or girlfriends, mostly behaving myself, but no one mentioned looking for love.

I found it interesting how friends and family treated me after my husband passed away. I sometimes felt like leftover mac and cheese perched on the second shelf of the refrigerator. They adjusted what and how they spoke to me, and as odd as it may seem, I became invisible, unable to be seen or heard. Loneliness set in and I felt unimportant and irrelevant, almost as if I, too, lay six feet under. Friends and family felt *uncomfortable talking to me, not knowing what to say or how to say it, preferring to say nothing, which left me even more alone. I interpreted their avoidance of me as not wanting to offend me or thinking I might burst into tears if they mentioned my husband. I wondered if they thought death was catching. Don't get too close; you might drop dead too.*

A death in the family is a complicated thing. Even if the family has experienced multiple deaths over the years, people are unsure how to handle a death of a loved one and, even more specifically, how to handle the remaining person. Relationships are altered, sometimes improved, other times damaged. There is a hole that hadn't been there before, and the filling in of that hole changes the entire family tapestry.

❧ *Robert's Story* ❦

Patty was a true matriarch, a bold female role model, and a super grandma. She led her grandchildren on adventure after adventure, and I was always glad to be in the support role. She and her sisters were close and kept in constant communication, even though they were a thousand miles away. Their support during her illness kept me buoyant and engaged. She was a religious person, strongly believing in God, and had many church friends. Her many friends from her aviation life were a huge help to her during her final days. A woman of many talents, she was a strong part of our family tapestry.

The family was so close to Patty that when she left, some seemed to separate from the tapestry, and I felt isolated and alone. As I struggled with grief and loneliness, the grandkids were supportive, and I began to rebuild myself and our tapestry bit by bit. Relationships had changed, and I began to cultivate closer relationships with my brothers and my son and daughter, which I admit I had not worked on much before.

But Wait! What Is Grandma Up to Now?

I arranged the funeral, the gravestone, and the graveside service. For the graveside service, I threw myself into the details, giving family members a role to play, making sure I left no one out. I included many of her friends in the active graveside service. I had dug the grave, her daughter read a eulogy, many of Patty's friends placed objects in the grave, and the grandkids each with a shovel filled the grave and buried their grandmother. Afterward we met at my home, and the visiting was grand with remembrances and laughter.

As I took my grandson's advice about tackling the online dating scene, my outlook improved and I became more positive, openly sharing my adventures with family. Unfortunately, this was not met with universal acceptance. The silence from parts of my family and friends was deafening. As I reflect on it now, I think that I did not pay enough attention in communicating my loneliness and grief, and therefore, they did not pick up on the signs that I was ready to move on and change.

In the present, the family tapestry is changed again; some holes have healed, some have drifted away, and some are closer. Meeting Gail added another family into our tapestry. I am just beginning to interact with her family, as I call it the "job interviews" of being her significant other. Both families have a role in my life, I like where I am, and I am more independent in thought and concern than I was before Patty's death. The adventure of life continues. I love having my family support and hope they enjoy our story, our united tapestry.

Emotions come without rules, and friends and family sometimes don't know what to say because they don't know how and what they feel. People have a wide range of emotions, spanning the emotional rainbow; then add elapsed time, and emotions may take on a life of their own. Long-past emotional memories may reappear out of nowhere and cause friction as people remember occasions and hurts that were unresolved and now reemerged as if they were from today. Sadness reigns, of course, but sometimes these other emotions may surface, altering how the widow, the widower, and the children of the deceased respond about the death of their loved one. Through our experience, we saw all of these, by a variety of people:

> **ANGER:** *Why did she have to die now?*
> **GUILT:** *I should have done more. I should have gone to see him.*
> **FORGIVENESS:** *She was terribly sick. I'm glad her suffering is over.*
> **LOVE:** *My heart is breaking.*
> **SELFISHNESS:** *He was mine. How could he have left me?*
> **CONCERN:** *What will happen next?*
> **CONFUSION:** *What will I do without him?*
> **RELIEF:** *Free of worry about her illness or health.*
> **EMPTINESS:** *How will we fill the space he left?*
> **HELPLESSNESS:** *Who's going to drive me to the doctor from now on?*
> **FEAR:** *It happened to him. I'm younger. Will it happen to me?*

To add to the confusion, instead of expressing feelings, family members may pocket them. They deny them and don't express their feelings to the person who needs help the most: the widow or widower, rather, leaving those closest to the death feeling left out and insignificant. Both of us felt isolated after the funerals; it was like they did their duty, time to resume life. This resumption seemed to omit the surviving spouse and our emotions, making conversations uncomfortable as we all tried to fit into new roles.

The tapestry of our family and close friends is not meant to constrain us, rather to provide support and comfort and help all of us through our grieving. Yet each of us is an individual person, unique in our thoughts and dreams, which are varied and may take us to adventures unknown or keep us in our own cocoon, secure and unchanging. Our children are our children, not our parents. As seniors, also known as the old folks or geezers, we need to take an active role in leading our family into this life change. We are filled with experience and wisdom and should have the foresight to mend the damage, heal the wounds, and lead our kids into the changing tapestry. But sometimes we don't get the chance. Their lives are busy, and our nightly phone calls seem to become a burden, a task, as they try to hurry through the call. Of course, that leaves us wondering what is next. Are we headed to the old folks' home, or as they say, "assisted living"? The insulation barrier placed between us and them is normal. The kids have no idea of loss except what they lost, a grandma or a grandpa, not what we lost, a lifelong friend, a lover, our business partner, and our soulmate. To reconcile these two viewpoints of loss is difficult, and with time, some normalcy in the family tapestry should appear, but it will never be the same.

So, what does this have to do with dating, or the idea of dating? We are alone yet interwoven into the tapestry of our network of family and friends, and we don't want to lose this network. Not only has the family experienced death and the changes in the relationships, but now Grandma or Grandpa is looking around, and the family is left with a dumbfounded look on their face. Dating? Grandma, are you thinking of dating? You are seventy years old. Are you kidding? This change is a double whammy because not only does the family have to deal with the death, but Grandma is also looking outside the family for love and companionship. Some family members may encourage Grandma, others not so much, or they may want to have input into Grandma's choice of a new roommate, like "I know this great poet who would be perfect."

Grandma says, "Grrr."

CHAPTER 10

INTERNET DATING: A NEW SOCK HOP

So here we are, full circle, back in our discussion of Internet dating. For those of us who have been labeled with a variety of monikers such as seniors, geezers, past our use-by date, or over the hill, it seems unrealistic to consider the idea of a date, especially using an online forum. But really, seniors are not much different from the young people of today. Through the ages, both generations have eyeballed the opposite sex while in junior high school, dated during high school, and became a little more serious at college, in a job, or in the military, finally settling into a match, hoping he or she was the right one to grow old with. When we were younger, we had no method of filtering out the wrong mates except our own common sense, coupled with nods of approval or disapproval from friends, family, or parents.

Officiants recite the phrase "until death do us part" at most marriage ceremonies, but we can agree that the sentiment isn't what it used to be. In America, annulment, separation, and divorce are commonplace, something we talk about easily. To the contrary, it is uncomfortable to think about what happens when someone dies. The early sitcoms like *Leave It to Beaver* and *Father Knows Best* defined family life as it was supposed to be. Later, sitcoms like *All in the Family* and *Sanford and Son* defined it differently, but still within the boundaries of relatively stable families. Our generation, back in our twenties, married young

Internet Dating: A New Sock Hop

and planned to be together for our entire lives. But now we see this isn't necessarily the case. As widowers and widows, we now enter a different world than what we knew as normal with few guidelines and boundaries.

❧ *Gail's Story* ❦

Two years after Tom died, the silence wore me down. I grew tired of being alone, tired of not having a good, healthy conversation about almost anything, and tired of wearing worn-out flannel pajamas when I crawled into bed. Cautiously, I called both of my lovely children and asked what they thought about my trying online dating. They met my question with a resounding silence, and even at the end of the phone call, I didn't know whether they approved or not. I wanted their buy-in and decided to give them a little time to adjust and come to me with their answer. They had lost their father, and I wasn't sure if they had moved through the grieving process as I had because they hadn't talked much about it. I tossed out the idea and told them to think about it. I'm not a patient person and began calling them both nightly, but wisely kept my real agenda to myself. I dutifully asked the family news, what they had done since I had called the day before, and asked for details about tomorrow's agenda. We have always been close, phone calls, lunches, and shopping, but the frequent conversations became strained as both grown kids remained silent.

I wanted to shout, "Hold it! I'm not dead! Pay attention!" but stuck a turnip in my mouth and kept quiet. Suddenly, everything I thought I believed about Internet dating was thrown to the wind. It would be an adventure, something new. It was also scary because I didn't know who might show up: an axe murderer, fortune hunter or just someone who wanted to teach me how to use the remote. On the one hand, I found the whole idea of finding another companion ridiculous because when

I fell in love with Tom, I knew I would never find another person like him. But on the other hand, I began to wonder if I might have room in my heart for another. Other people had. Why not me? And did I need to have my kids give me their okay?

One day while I was feeling sorry for myself as I lamented their lack of interest in me, it hit me like a lightning bolt. My children were in their forties, in their prime earning years, with people to see and fires to extinguish. They had lives of their own to live, and my poor-me nightly phone calls and the why-can't-you-go-to-lunch-with-me whining alienated me from what had always been a comfortable relationship. They didn't have time to think about me or online dating or axe murderers. I needed to continue to figure it out on my own.

I knew a couple of people who had online dated, and I reviewed my email contact list and thought of a couple more. Henry, who lives down the street, said he met Melinda online, but it had been years ago, and besides, it might be different for men. And then I remembered the cute couple at church, Sam and Naomi. They hold hands all during the service, except when they go to communion. I know they met online. And we met Gloria and Glenn on a cruise a couple of years ago. They were in their sixties and seemed happy, even joyful, about their mates. Maybe there were more online couples than I thought.

I had grown tired of waiting for my children to come to their senses and glanced at my computer screen and decided to continue forging ahead. My granddaughter had sort of encouraged me. "You should try it, Grandma. It's all the rage with old people. You can go online and maybe you'll find a hunk of burnin' love, like that Elvis guy." I laughed as I thought of her and her innocence and filled out another profile, taking more care this time, adding a better picture, one I had found of me on a ship crossing the Panama Canal, and hit enter.

Internet Dating: A New Sock Hop

You Aren't Computer Savvy, You Say?

The first computer dating sites appeared in 1959 when a pair of college students linked up classmates, about fifty young women and fifty young men, but the real computerized matching of people with computer-driven data was sporadic until about 1995, when several Internet dating sites took off and began their task of matching people up. According to Wikipedia, 40 percent of married couples have met online.

By 1995, we baby boomers were steaming past age fifty and beginning to slow our careers or even retire. Computers had become commonplace, and some careers required the ability to use them, but others needed less computer knowledge and ability, meaning many baby boomers never learned how to use a computer. Even though the idea of putting our personal information on a website concerns us (correction: it scares the living daylights out of us), we have learned to bank online, search for housing, and order from Amazon. We got this!

In the 1980s, most people met their mates through friends, at work, or church. Friends engaged in a sort of matchmaking and introduced their unmarried friends to someone they thought had possibilities. The matchmaking process worked fine before we became dependent on computers, but now the dominant dating tool is online dating, and this usage has increased in popularity by leaps and bounds, jumping from 20 to 40 percent in just ten years, 2010–20. And multiple research studies confirm that many seniors have realized its potential and have hopped on board.

Many people of a certain age still don't have computer skills or are not inclined to admit their inability to use a computer, fearful of being labeled "a dinosaur," but it's not true. Asking for help in this computerized world may send you on the fast track toward a younger and fuller lifestyle. Anyone can solve the lack of computer skills, which is nothing to be ashamed of. After all, today's millennials don't have a clue about slide rules. Think of it this way: If you give online dating a whirl, not only will you have the adventure of meeting someone, but you also will smooth out those gray-matter wrinkles and crinkles and cause your grandkids to cheer their tech-savvy grandma with high-fives. "Look at Grandma go!"

The dating pool is huge, with at least 300,000 people going online each month and many more options than we had while sitting behind a dreamboat in our high school math class. Through the miracle of technology, we can sit at home behind a computer screen, looking at a half-a-million silver-haired dreamboats, age sixty-five to seventy-five and beyond.

Now That We've Got You Thinking...

So maybe you're considering Internet dating but wonder who would ever look at you. You notice you have bulges and wrinkles and don't look as nice or sexy as you wish, and what person in his or her right mind would take a second glance. As we noted earlier, we simply feel old and saggy, with gray hair and wrinkles that are…well, you know, too many to count. Wrinkle creams don't work, and wrinkles remain right where we least want them.

That paragraph sounds like a woman wrote it, but a man is no less vain than a woman. Both sexes gaze in the mirror and say, "What happened? Who is that old gal or guy in the mirror? My mother? Or my father?" Some things are fixable, like losing weight, learning to dance, beefing up the underused pecs at the gym, but an over-seventy-year-old body is what it is. Creaks, gray hair, and wrinkles aren't going anywhere. Well, guess what? All of us on the dating sites are in the same boat! You just need to take a look!

Internet Dating: A New Sock Hop

Sure, your physical appearance is important, and it is crucial to emphasize your strengths, which might not be the image that reflects in the mirror. Remember, a photograph and a few details are all that describe you on a dating site. Be easy on yourself. In our age range, most of us worry about how we look, and if you think about it, it is not much different than that senior high sock hop where all the girls lined up on one side of the gym with identical poodle skirts and bouffant hairdos, and the boys all looked like James Dean, white T-shirts, blue jeans, and ducktails. It was fun then and it is fun now.

The problem with staring into the mirror is that the future and potential are missing from the image. Although we have experienced a lifetime of knowledge and excitement, tomorrow and beyond are absent. We know what we would like them to be, but they don't reflect in the mirror, for example, the good times lying just around the corner, the laughter of two people enjoying each other, or the joy emerging as we launch new adventures. We only see the image reflecting our outside appearance today, not the twinkle in our eyes or the songs in our heart or the spring in our step, all of which are hiding just beneath the surface, ready to make an appearance the moment we begin a new adventure, meet new people, and try new outlets.

Our potential dancing partner has the same insecurities and regrets the lumps and bumps, life scars, thinning gray hair, liver spots, or even the missing breast from a long-gone cancer battle. These are part of who we are and have made us the person we are. No one who is seventy has the perfect body, face, or brain.

On the other hand, we've all known people covered with wrinkles, yet their spirit and outlook on life are the same as when they were younger. They think young, accept new people and ideas easily, and are excited to get up in the morning, looking forward to the adventures the new day might hold. They seem proud of their wrinkles and view them as proof of wisdom, experience, or energy instead of aging. The swashbuckling, never-look-back spirit comes from inside, from the brain, a direct link to how they view the world.

Dating site technology helps us see possibilities. We can study a photograph, read a profile, and gather clues about a life history. This person has already lived over a half century with a full life, and the Internet can help us look beyond what we see on the screen and reveal potential and a future. Hitting "send" is like going to the sock hop, walking across that floor to that guy or gal who has caught your eye. Maybe she'll say yes, maybe no, and it's the same in the Internet world. Take a chance, select a thumbs-up, a wink, and hit send.

❧ Robert's Story ❧

After my grandson laid down the law to stop wallowing in misery and get on with life, I cranked up the old computer and started researching. This felt like unchartered territory, and now I had a mission. I knew a bit about computers and looked at this as planning for an action-packed trip, but I didn't know where it was going to take me. I am an engineer/mechanic by training, and I like to know how things work. I decided to research widowers online and tried to learn what it meant to be a widower and what I could expect as time passed. Would I ever have a prospect of meeting women or having a date? Would I be wasting my time?

I located several dating websites and found author Abel Keogh, who seemed particularly relatable. He was a widower and wrote books about widowhood. The dating sites filled in my lack of knowledge about myself as a potential dating person and my status as a seventy-six-year-old widower. I learned which feelings were normal and read a few dating scenarios as well as some reviews. I discovered a lot about myself, what other men felt, and the normalcy of my roller-coaster emotions. I

Internet Dating: A New Sock Hop

discovered grieving had no time limit, nor did the search for companionship. I could define my expectations of what I wanted from a relationship, whether she would be a friend, a companion, or someone I wanted to wake up next to for the rest of my life. This period of introspection gave me some time to think about who I was, a mid-seventies widower in good health with a sense of adventure. I thought about sex, of course, and the websites affirmed my feelings were normal. Whew! What a relief.

So, my education continued, and I considered what I really wanted. I missed the romance, flowers, and other nice things a man does for his wife or lover and realized in the last twenty years I had fallen to neglecting those romantic gestures, which I now, since she died, regretted as much as anything. I should have flirted more and spent more time on the little things, and I told myself, "That mistake won't happen again." I decided to enjoy all of life's pleasures, smiles, hugs, and small romantic things like eye contact and subtle touching. I wanted strong intimacy, whether intellectual, emotional, or physical. I wanted a partner I could romance and make smile and laugh. I hoped for sex, but that wasn't my driving force, rather companionship, adventure, and romance. I hoped to find someone who wanted the same.

I knew I hadn't laughed in a long time. I knew that laughter banishes silence, and the thought of laughing again spun up this old cowboy. I imagined meeting my silver-haired vixen, sharing coffee and laughter again, and then where would this lead? To Paris? Walking down the Seine banks, like lovers had for hundreds of years? I love Paris and have high hopes and dreams! The whole idea of going to Paris with a new love got my juices boiling! Damn the torpedoes, boys, this is going to be fun!

So, I got busy researching dating sites, sorting through them before realizing most were geared to people under forty, younger than my grandkids. I saw words like "profiles" and "psychological matching" along with words like "catfishing" and "ghosting." I recognized that, like life, when you see the whole picture, you learn there is the good and the bad. I remember my dad talking about con men as I became a teenager, so this dark side did not surprise me. "Eyes wide open," I told myself as a man in his seventies who was simply looking for meaningful conversation, some love, and romance. I was forewarned and decided to start the search again with a bit more care. I filtered the sites with "over seventy, widowed" and looked for websites that could deliver on those basic terms. I found six websites that were recognized as reliable with positive reviews and set those six as my start on a grand adventure. I initially joined SilverSingles.com and paid the money for a ninety-day run. A few days later I added FarmersOnly.com because I am a rancher and liked the idea of meeting someone with similar interests. My niece took a good picture of me, and I completed the profiles and added my picture to the sites and started my adventure. Wahoo! Let's see what happens!

I don't know what an algorithm is, and I don't know who to ask.

Internet dating is nothing more than a modern matchmaking system. Instead of a yenta, it uses algorithms that provide a level of accuracy far superior to what a simple marriage broker or dating coach might use. An algorithm is loosely defined as computer-generated problem solving in geek speak. It is another term that we don't fully understand, but we shrugged and thought, *Millions of men and women are doing this. If they can do it, we can too.* As we dug deeper, we learned that the digital matchmaking system provides mega opportunities to pair couples, with a reasonably good degree of success. Some dating sites do not use these algorithm processes and still manage to be successful in their matchmaking.

Matchmaking is not new, certainly, as matchmakers have been around for centuries, scrutinizing people's potential and making matches. Matchmakers and dating or relationship coaches try to see what can be, the potential for a good link-up between two lonely people and emerging

Internet Dating: A New Sock Hop

laughter, accepting or ignoring the past. Technology asks the questions, the user enters the answers into a profile, and away you go. The profile combined with technology can give us a better understanding about this potential match. This information then allows us to compare Match A (Andrea) with Match B (Betty) with Match C (Carol), and with those comparisons, we can choose our future, hopefully a perfect match. It gives us the information to help make an informed choice.

We all have been on a blind date and loved it or hated it. Internet dating is a blind date on steroids except we can choose the blind date from a long list of possibilities. We can add personal choices or requirements, like non-smoker, non-drinker, over six feet tall, or rhumba dancers with extensive knowledge of raising chickens, and the computer program will filter those choices. And because Internet websites require photos, we know what they look like. Internet dating sites also ask a few questions, and the profile presented by the prospective match allows you to take a look around before you choose.

Remember back in the days when we all diligently read local newspapers and people took out personal classified ads? The ad would read *SBF wants energetic SBM for conversation and companionship. Must be able to cook or play golf and enjoy children. Call this number.* They were popular when newspapers were popular, but today printed newspapers have largely been replaced by the Internet, where we can access information twenty-four hours a day, seven days a week. So, Internet dating? Why not? Take a photo, write a profile, turn on the computer, and watch the fun begin.

CHAPTER 11

Strut Your Stuff

We've already established that a sense of adventure and lighthearted energy need to be a part of online dating, but we are trapped inside seventy-year-old bodies with similarly aged brains, which can cause a problem. Recapturing the spirit of our youth might not seem easy, but if we are determined, we can demonstrate the sense of adventure we once had. Instead of acting younger, we can show we are young "at heart," portraying a positive image, optimism, and energy.

Just like a toothpaste commercial, you are selling yourself, with two specific ways of doing this in online dating: photos and profiles.

Photo, Are You Sure?

Your photo is the first thing someone will see as they scroll through their "matches," making it the most important part of your profile. For many of us, the thought of having a photo taken sends shivers down our spines. Our bodies are not exactly what we think of as perfect, with sags, bags, and dark spots on parts of our bodies that we used to emphasize as our best feature. In our research, we have viewed hundreds of photos and collected a bucketful of knowledge and opinions about what creates a good photo for a dating site. With the new iPhone technology, you can

Strut Your Stuff

be anyone you like, any age or color of hair, even with or without teeth. A bald person can have hair, a bushy haired person can be bald, hats can be added or subtracted, but the best advice we offer is to be yourself. Everyone has flaws. After all, we are experienced with wisdom from years of doing "stuff," and each little flaw has a story, so smile, make good conversation, and enjoy the ride.

Your photo should be one of you alone, showing off your best assets, especially your eyes and your smile, but also your personality. Taboo are sunglasses, hats, and gaudy jewelry, anything that hides the real you. Technology has given us selfies, and they might be okay in some cases, but you will be better off to ask someone to take your photo, a close-up, clear, not blurred, showing your best assets, eyes and smile for sure, but maybe your physique. Professional photos aren't always expensive, especially if you go to a store specializing in passport photos or a local photo shop. The photo should be of you alone, not with your sister or friend. Pets are okay too, if they are incidental, but the picture should be of you, not your pets. And it must be current. You would be surprised how many people post their high school graduation photo or king-or-queen-of-the-hop photo from fifty years ago. Men, you should have shirts on and buttoned. Women, consider the color and style of your shirt or sweater, classic or something eye-catching, even flirty, but don't get carried away! And please don't lie on a pillow, your beautiful hair cascading behind you, with half-open eyes. You might think it looks sexy, but it may give a different impression than you want to give, or it could look like you are staging for a coffin shot, a definite turnoff. Some sites reject photos with children, meaning photos with grandchildren, although cute, are no-nos. Just you and you, alone.

Photoshopping has recently emerged to create an image whose appearance and complexion are flawless. It covers up a lot of sins, including wrinkles, crinkles, and double chins. But it's not real. Showing off the real you and emphasizing those attributes with makeup, stylish outfits, and the right kind of lighting will make for a better photo and a more honest presentation of yourself. Eyes open and don't forget to smile!

Also, think about the backdrop of your photo. What will demonstrate your interests and energy? Which would be better, reclining in your easy chair, watching the news, or smiling at the array of flowers from your garden? Sitting in your car, smiling and waving at someone, or a selfie in your bedroom mirror with the phone blocking your face? Laughing at your pet's antics or reading a book? Think of something interesting or fun and always present yourself with a happy countenance. Most good pictures we take are accidental, so ask your grandkids to snap some good shots of you while you are busy being you, and then sort them out to find the best ones. Try to put at least three different photos on the site with different outfits, different settings, doing different activities, always smiling. Remember, you are trying to catch the eye of someone. The subject of the photo is you, not the car, horse, motorcycle, or your cute puppy.

Pictures of people holding a string of fish seem popular, as do pictures of people sitting on motorcycles. Perhaps that is your target, and if so, go for it. Emphasize your passions, which will help to increase those matches who really do align with your profile. Pictures of family gatherings or with your deceased spouse are also taboo, as are cartoon emojis and avatars. Some people post photos holding hands with their deceased spouse, and this is a definite no-no. Although you might think you are honoring your deceased mate, it could be a turnoff to someone new.

Spend the time finding a photo fitting you. You want to look brave and attractive, full of energy, optimism, and pride. Think beyond the picture and consider how it will be perceived by the online potential match.

Profile, or What the Heck Have You Done for Seventy-five Years...

A profile is the second thing a potential match looks at. Just like the toothpaste commercial, the words complement the visual, the photo. Your profile creates a more complete picture and explanation of who you are. You know who you are, but you want your match to know enough about you to spark an interest, a flicker, and perhaps a flame as he/she pauses at your photo—as well as dozens of other potential matches.

A profile needs to tell two stories: who you are and how you have used this wonderful life. But it also needs to identify what you are looking for in another person or relationship. You can be general or specific, but be realistic and remember you will be searching for someone who is as wise and experienced as you are. Every dating site asks its own profile questions, and you should carefully consider what you are trying to accomplish before you answer them. Answer the questions fully and truthfully, and don't leave any gaps if possible. You might not want to discuss your religious faith or political views, but whether you have children is a simple question, as are marital status, drinking alcohol, and smoking because they are "deal breakers" for some matches. In this real-life example below, no real information is furnished, and it sparks no interest for the reader. Perhaps the writer thought himself or herself coy, hard to catch, but we saw them as trying to hide something. The reader comes away with no more information than he/she had when he/she saw the photo.

This is an actual example of a set of dating site profile questions and the real, knock-your-socks-off answers, but don't use it as a guide. Do not follow this example!

LOVING AGAIN

- *What is your marital status?*   *I'll tell you later.*
- *Do you want children?*   *I'll tell you later.*
- *What is your level of education?*   *I'll tell you later.*
- *Do you have children?*   *No kids.*
- *What is your religious faith?*   *I'll tell you later.*
- *What is your body type?*   *I'll tell you later.*
- *Do you drink alcohol?*   *I'll tell you later.*
- *Do you smoke?*   *I'll tell you later.*
- *How tall are you?*   *5'7".*
- *What city do you live in?*   *I'll tell you later.*

What is he hiding? Was he in a time crunch? Was he unsure of the answers? Really? This profile went to Gail, and it said nothing to indicate who he was or why she should or should not pursue him. He wanted to tell her later but didn't scratch enough surface trust to earn a "later," and she swiped left as she puzzled what his answers meant. The questions are easy and certainly don't require an answer, but remember, this whole exercise is to capture someone's attention for a conversation or a date. Your prospective match looks your text over as the first tangible information about you and can swipe left, "delete," or continue. Give your answers some thought and make them interesting and enticing.

The normal questions on the profile page are varied. Some sites have a full array of questions, everything from soup to nuts with no apparent order. Some sites ask only a few questions, but all sites will have these five questions, phrased differently.

What are you looking for? Conversation Commitment Compatibility Long-Term Relationship

ADVICE: If you aren't sure, mark conversation. It won't lock you into anything more than a good cup of coffee and a conversation.

What age range are you looking for?
50-60   60-70   70-80   80+

ADVICE: Mark the age closest to your own age, as you will have most in common with them. If you are on the cusp, mark "both" if the website allows it; otherwise, choose the one you prefer. Remember, older does not mean richer or needing caregiving, and younger does not mean energy or someone who is working. It simply means someone who is about your age, reared in the same decade.

What marital status are you looking for?
Never married   Separated   Divorced   Widowed

ADVICE: If you are widowed, mark "widowed." We have found widows and widowers are more likely to view a relationship as a bond. For some, however, it doesn't matter. The heart will dictate what's next!

What location are you looking for?
Within 10 miles   50 miles   100 miles   200 miles

ADVICE: Mark appropriately. If you live in a rural area, mark a longer distance. If you live in a city, mark the shorter distance. This will largely depend on your available means of transportation and how you see this relationship developing. If only for an occasional date, a longer trip may be okay, but if you are truly interested in a long-term relationship, consider the ramifications of distance and transportation. In our case, we started at six hundred miles, met at three hundred miles, and now we have moved in together. You never know!

What ethnicity or race or religion are you interested in? (Usually three questions)

ADVICE: Think about these. No one is going to call you a racist or bigot, but be sure you are comfortable with how you mark. The fourth social issue that may appear is politics. Figure out your own biases and how you will ask or answer if a political question arises, and it will arise.

Life or lifestyle questions

ADVICE: Answers will be varied, but no matter what your reason for online dating, it is important to be positive, even eager, and put your best energy-filled foot forward. You have had a life of experiences, pleasures, as well as problems. Turn them into an interesting story. Isn't it more fun to be involved with someone with energy and a sense of adventure than a couch potato who never smiles? Give it your best shot, then read it aloud and rework it. Everyone has had bad things happen throughout their life, but there is no reason to dwell on it. A new romance will give you a new lease on life.

SUGGESTION: Take a good look at the questions before answering and write out your answers on a piece of paper before submitting them to the website. Make sure you haven't omitted any words, made any errors, using complete sentences, good grammar, and proper spelling, for sure, but also your thoughts about your past and future. It never hurts to have a friend check it over. Review your answers to be sure they are positive and interesting.

Part of your profile may be an essay, open-ended, where you describe yourself in your own words. You should spend some quality time writing your profile essay, your likes and dislikes, to create an image of yourself telling your best qualities and your outlook on life.

As you write something about your likes and dislikes, include what kinds of things you like to do but not your life story. Include the highlights, like hometown and school information, but not your relationship with your parents or how often you moved or your superior or failing grades. Spend enough time to make your answers complete, maybe a couple of paragraphs, and something that makes the reader smile. Make them upbeat, not beat-up. Adding a flirty comment might be fun too, such as "I love receiving flowers, especially from blue-eyed cowboys." Or "Walking along the banks of the Danube in the moonlight holding my lover's hand is my favorite fantasy. What is your favorite fantasy?" If you haven't flirted or been flirted with in a long time, think about how it excited you when you were younger. Now might be the time to try your hand at a flirty note.

What are you looking for? The profile should also explain what you are looking for in a relationship. Maybe you don't know exactly what you want in your quest for online dating, but this is your time to expand on your preferences, and it is good to review your own likes and dislikes. As a widowed person, it is important to think about the type of person you are interested in. You've already had a successful union and get to choose something similar or something different. Are you interested in someone who will take the place of that person, or are you in the market for conversation, companionship, or a Valentine's Day date? Are you looking for someone who is different from your past spouse or someone similar? What is important to you as you look for a possible life partner? Appearance, race, religion, politics, age, health, interests are all up for grabs. You can apply filters that will include or exclude people who don't fit your standards, but there are many other filters, like pets, temperament, sports, music, entertainment. The list can be endless. What's on yours?

A good, well-thought-out, and well-presented profile can lead to all kinds of adventures, including the more serious, the "s-e-x" word, an option, but not a requirement. Would you prefer an occasional phone call, lunch date, or somebody to take a drive with? Or a meaningful discussion and somewhat heated debate about the politics of the day over coffee? Would you be open to a special Friday night date? Or are you looking for a longer-term relationship, to include trips and holidays and gatherings of friends and family, showing the two of you as a "couple" or an "item"? Would you like indulging in a platonic dinner cruise down a river with a good friend whom you met online, or do you have an intense fear of water and boating?

Below are four real-life examples of poorly written, poorly thought-out essays.

Real-Life Example #1: In A Nutshell *life is great the only thng that can make it better is to enjoy it with somebody the rest of the way to walk in to the sun set side by side*

The One I Am Looking For
- *not sure that i am looking for anything in partcular*
- *just would enjoy getting to meet you and find our mutual intrest and see where life leads us*
- *I'd Just Like to Add*
- *i enjoy working in the yards dancing kisses and hugs travel a nice glass of wine and where ever we are at the time lifes is to short to worry over much any more*

ADVICE: THE SENTIMENTS ARE WONDERFUL, BUT PLEASE CHECK SPELLING AND GRAMMAR

Real-Life Example #2: *i am retire from work for a long time   I collected die car long time i over 3oo*

ADVICE: SHOW ENTHUSIASM, SPELLING, GRAMMAR

Real-Life Example #3: *I'm looking for a lady who has no problem with me being disabled. I don't think that I am all that interesting.*

ADVICE: BECOME INTERESTING! SHOW OFF YOUR GOOD POINTS

Real-Life Example #4: *I have a great sense of humor and like to chat about various subjects. I am married but it seems we don't have much in common anymore.*

ADVICE: READ THE PROFILE. IF YOU DON'T, WHO KNOWS WHAT YOU WILL FIND! REMEMBER *FATAL ATTRACTION*? HIDE THE RABBITS!

The goal of presenting a great photo and a powerful profile is to find a "match" on a website that leads to an FDA, nothing more, a look-see at the other person, eyeballing him/her, finding out if you like how he/she looks and presents himself/herself, and whether you might have a meaningful conversation, crucial to intimacy, albeit intellectual intimacy. But on an FDA, if things go well, you might decide to have a second or third date adventure. Pick your site, paste that photo, complete the profile, and join in the Internet dance!

CHAPTER 12

The Eight-Thousand-Site Question

Once we decided to write our book, and believe us, it was no small decision, we likened it to trying to remove a bee from a bowl of honey as we selected the sites that would work for us. Fantasies of love and romance maxed out our brains, especially as the website descriptions promised all this "for just a few cents a day." Holy guacamole, we thought, were they all making empty promises, or could we believe what they said? How in the world can a person choose one dating site over another? They all look and sound alike.

In our quest for finding the best online dating sites for seniors, we researched dozens of websites and their reviews, both the popular sites and the lesser-known ones. We are both seniors with varying experiences in online dating, and we met by accident. Robert had paid for three sites while Gail joined one free site for only a few days as she researched a book, but by good fortune, we met.

For our testing, we decided to submit identical profile parameters, that of senior citizens aged sixty-eight to seventy-eight years old, widowed, within two hundred miles of our homes, located in two different states, Idaho and Montana. (A long distance to date, but

Idaho and Montana are large in area.) The information we presented was factual about us and our lives, no lies or exaggerations. We reviewed many sites, then chose the six highest-rated ones meeting all our parameters, later adding FarmersOnly because of the rural nature of our states. They were mainstream dating sites with many reviews, and they allowed our selection criteria. We anticipated that the age category of "seniors" would be the easiest, but it became the most difficult. Some sites set the senior category at age fifty years old or even forty, and many did not acknowledge that people over sixty-five years would be interested in dating. We chose not to use those sites. Safety concerns were high on our list but were not filters; rather we watched and scrutinized site standards. Our own experiences in dating divorcees and never-marrieds confirmed our thoughts that widows and widowers view life and love differently from divorcees. Being widowed, we understand that losing a spouse through death generates mixed emotions, different from those of the divorced or never-married persons. In addition, as a caregiver for a deceased spouse, our memories and feelings are difficult, maybe even impossible, for the divorced or never-married person to understand. We don't mean to insinuate that older divorced persons cannot be a good match, but narrowing the selection to the widowed category may make the match of a long-term soulmate more successful.

Michele Kearns, in her website JoyReturns.com, noted that widows and widowers are aware of how quickly life can change and appreciate the little things in their lives. Widows and widowers understand a passion for living and can easily involve themselves in new and different things. Widows and widowers have already passed through a stormy period and understand the sun will once again rise if they just give it a chance.

We joined seven websites for research purposes, being careful not to answer the matches or lead someone on by any kind of response. We wanted to know:

A. How the website worked.
B. What algorithm system was used, that is, how they do the matchmaking.
C. The difficulty and barriers for joining a dating site.
D. The costs and lengths of commitment.
E. How our parameters matched the responses we received.
F. Safety considerations advocated by the sites.

One dating site phenomenon for seniors is the lopsided number of each gender; many more women than men are on the sites. According to statista.com and the U.S. Department of Health and Human Services, over eleven million widows and widowers over the age of sixty-five lived in the U.S. in 2020. Those numbers break down to three and a half million men and over eight million women, about a three-to-one ratio of widowed women to widowed men, and the online dating sites for seniors reflect this bias. This reminds us of the old saying "Women mourn, men replace."

The actual dating site ratios are about 44 percent male and 56 percent female for the senior or over-fifty age group, as defined by AARP. As the age group moves toward seventy, the ratios also move, becoming 40 percent male and 60 percent female, perhaps because of men's lower life expectancy.

The sites we discuss are in order of our preference, but all these sites are mainstream, reputable, and have built-in safeguards, which we identify. We ranked these sites as we would use them. If it took longer than drinking a cup of coffee to join, had complex technology, or the

The Eight-Thousand-Site Question

free trial offer did not sell us, we ranked them lower. Reviews can be a good tool, but as we read them, we realized many reviewers are millennials or younger persons and have different goals and outlooks than we silver-haired foxes and vixens. They may want a "hookup," which means a one-night stand, a different date nightly, or they seek a fast track to love. Sometimes they are in a hurry, and if they aren't happy within a week, they want their money back. Check the reviews, but don't bet your life's savings on the reviewers' comments.

We do not advise getting on any old dating website just because it sounds cute. According to *Forbes*, more than eight thousand dating sites float throughout the world. On a whim Gail joined one of these "cute" sites, and after joining, an unknown guy hacked into her phone number and figured out where she lived and what she did for a living, all from the data on their website—nothing she had entered herself. This meant that she had to change passwords and user IDs and void a credit card. That site offered no protective standards.

The Internet has plenty of off-ramps taking you into places you don't want to go, meaning you must be alert. We believe our listed sites are reputable and should be fine, but if you have any creepy feelings, cancel the site and get out. If you feel your credit card has been compromised, call the credit card company immediately and ask to cancel the card. For that reason, we suggest sites allowing or even encouraging you to look around for free, paying later if the site appeals to you. Despite what they say and the multiple requests for payment, they will let you stay on the site for many days, even weeks, without paying.

Paying for a site allows you to share and view your matches with more detail, and after your free look-around, we suggest joining one or two sites that appeal to you for the minimum amount of time, usually three months, about $20-$40 per month. You should look at this as an investment and can reasonably expect to meet someone, but the sites offer no guarantees.

If all goes well, you should have some good text conversations within the site in a couple of days, perhaps even a couple of hours! Being within the site means that your identity and phone number are shielded, not released, until you agree to share with your texting partner. This is a good thing. When you later agree to allow texting to your phone number, this may lead to an in-person conversation or a date. If you do find "the one," don't ask for your money back, because it was an investment, but you should cancel the membership to avoid leading someone else on. Take extra measures to verify the site cancelled your membership, checking both the site and your credit card account, even if you must do it on the phone with a live agent.

Although sites often recommend it, committing to a long-term payment plan as the "best deal" is probably not the "best deal." Resist joining for an entire year on your first try, even though a longer-term commitment might seem less expensive by the month. An entire year is a big financial investment, and you may find "the one" on your first try or discover something in the site that turns you off. Remember, this is a contract, and if you exit the site and decide to quit, the annual commitment is still due.

Now You Are Scaring Me. So What's Really True? Myths and Facts about Online Dating

Online dating can be either dangerous or safe, and you must take the precautions. Daytime talk shows and coffee shop chatter offer as many myths as you want to hear, but evidence from studies indicates that online dating is no more dangerous than meeting someone in a grocery store and much less dangerous than in a bar.

The Eight-Thousand-Site Question

With eight thousand sites available, the availability of matches is almost beyond belief. Safety should remain our top priority, requiring us to look at each site for its safety features along with ease of use and compatibility for our individual search needs. Based on our experience and research, our top-rated sites are safe, or as safe as we can normally expect from the online world. We rank these sites with no compensation or benefit of any kind from site owners. We must remember the younger generation, millennials (born between 1981 and 1996), have a much wider understanding of the Internet than we seniors do and build most of the dating sites. Perhaps they don't concern themselves with the safety aspect, but we seniors are concerned about safety and have the advantage of experience and judgment. Our experiences have taught us things those youngsters haven't encountered yet, and we approach these sites with built-in caution.

"I would never do online dating. It is way too dangerous," said a silver-haired lady to Gail. "Oprah and Dr. Phil had programs about all the bad things that happen to women, and great balls of fire, terrible people are online, waiting to steal my money, rape, or even kill me."

This comment often comes from a person who never has tried online dating, and yes, all kinds of terrible things can happen to us in either the online world or the offline world. Many serious things occur every day on or off the Internet. Most of us know how to stay safe, locking our doors at night, hanging up on the robo-caller who is determined to sell us a condo, not answering the guy named Potential Spam who wants to renew our automobile warranty on a car we sold years ago. We know better than to share our credit card or bank information, except when we order online and throw caution out the window. We are aware of risky behaviors and manage them without ever thinking twice about them. We know which precautions to take and can calculate risks based on our life experiences and common sense, but still, we occasionally get burned.

Most of the time we enjoy life without fear, but we understand the fact that evil people are in our world. Our common sense and experience tell us when to raise our concern and the shivers up our spine are valid.

❧ Robert's Story ☙

When I first started to online date, I researched the top seven-rated websites before I subscribed to three, all of which showed a favorable history and positive reviews. I first subscribed to two, then added a third. I wanted to meet a silver-haired vixen older than seventy, widowed, not divorced, who had an interesting profile and whom I could see having a cup of coffee with and, if things went well, waking up next to her for the rest of my life. I met interesting people, and their conversations and texts enriched my life daily.

Of my thirty or more actual contacts over a six-month period, only one turned into a scam. She claimed to live in a neighboring state, Wyoming, but I wondered because her area code was from New York State. We texted within the app sporadically, and I learned she worked in the jewelry business. One day she asked if I could help her out; her jewelry shipment had been held up in customs, and she needed $500 because her funds were tied up in her inventory. $500? No way. I immediately blocked her, then cancelled the credit card I used to subscribe to this site and felt a shiver down my spine as if touched by a vampire.

Here are a few commonsense practices that all sites agree on:

- Free dating sites have less security; one in ten users on free sites are "scammers" according to DatingAdvice.com. Stay with the major sites and check the safety statements. This does not apply to a major site you are trying on for free.

The Eight-Thousand-Site Question

- If your prospective match displays these in text, avoid them:
  - *Extremely poor grammar*
  - *Obvious spelling errors*
  - *Lack of pictures*
  - *Any pictures that don't fit the age of the person*
  - *Over-the-top flattery in early conversation (Gail even got a marriage proposal!)*
  - *Any mention of money or request for financial help*

- Keep your phone number private until you are ready to share with your new friend. GPS tracking is a sneaky way to stalk, so be wary of sharing your phone number. However, perhaps enabling your phone's GPS tracking function to allow a friend or family to track you on your FDA would be a good idea for obvious reasons. If you don't know how to do this, ask your grandchild or teenaged neighbor. Some dating sites use your phone number to verify your identity, which is a good security feature for site users, and we like it because it cuts down on phony phone numbers and identities, aka "catfishing." It's a good idea to verify the site's security features and guarantee your phone number remains private.

The FBI takes complaints about these and other cybercrimes at its Internet Crime Complaint Center. They offer this guidance:

- Be careful what you post online. Scammers can use details from social media and dating sites to target you.
- Research a person's photo and profile online. Check if the image, name, or details have been used elsewhere. You can search photos via images.google.com.

- If you meet a prospective partner, go slowly, and ask lots of questions.
- Beware if the individual seems too perfect or quickly asks you to leave a dating service or social media site to communicate directly.
- Beware if the individual attempts to isolate you from friends and family or requests inappropriate photos or financial data that could be used to extort you.
- Beware if the individual promises to meet in person but always has an excuse about why he or she can't. If you haven't met the person after a few months, you have good reason to be suspicious.
- If someone you met online needs your bank account information to deposit money, they are most likely using your account for other thefts and frauds.

Our Top Seven Dating Sites

We chose seven sites for our testing with the filters we noted above, with safety, ease of use, cost and length of sign-up obligation all in mind. These sites were well-documented and well used and rated high by several Internet dating site reviewers. We give our opinions and suggestions and, at times, quote other reviewers, and we attribute those reviewers. Our rankings are recommendations for the senior population, and we listed our preferences in order, ranking them by our experiences in joining the sites, the number of matches, and the relevancy of the matches.

The Eight-Thousand-Site Question

The rankings in our order of preference are:

- *ChristianMingle.com*
- *OurTime.com*
- *Match.com*
- *SilverSingles.com*
- *EliteSingles.com*
- *eHarmony.com*
- *FarmersOnly.com*

ChristianMingle.com

Christian Mingle has fifteen million members, and if a Christian, faith-based relationship is important, this site is for you. In our testing, it was one of the fastest and easiest to join, with a five- to ten-minute sign-up, and for those of us who are not fans of computers, this may be one of the easiest sites to join.

Christian Mingle is among the largest dating sites in the industry. It caters to Christian men and women and has excellent search filters and safety features. Several dating site reviewers reported this was the most popular women's dating site, and we think the safety measures may factor into this statistic. This site allows users to specify widow or widower in their preferences. Although it is entitled "Christian Mingle," we did not find that it pushed religion or faith to its subscribers.

Christian Mingle has been around for about twenty years. You can cancel your membership after only one month but will not receive a refund for the current subscription term. You may start out with a free test drive and then join if it appeals to you.

In our testing, as free users, Robert had over forty "matches" in the first two days. Gail had eighteen. This seems to confirm the bias of more women than men on this site. Nearly 59 percent of the users are female, and 41 percent are male. The geographic locations of our matches fell generally within the two-hundred-mile criteria set, and the ages generally met our sixty-eight to seventy-eight age range. We set a widow/widower preference, and most matches fell within those parameters with only a few who were divorced, indicating the function was useful.

The safety features, the ease of joining, and the response rate caused us to list this site as our favorite.

- **Site Name**: ChristianMingle.com
- **Paid or Free**: Paid membership site with a free trial
- **Average Sign-Up Time**: 5-10 minutes, depending on if you complete your profile or not
- **Paid Membership Pricing**: Memberships start at $24.99 per month, with a three-month minimum.
- **Unique Christian Mingle Facts and Figures**:
  - The dating community is fifteen million strong.
  - Christian Mingle is regularly regarded by most as the number one Christian dating site. (Please note the Internet offers many other faith-based sites but may or may not offer the same information and safety features entered here.)
  - You can access your account through the mobile-friendly website or through the iPhone or Google Play apps.
  - The community has existed for nearly two decades starting in 2001.
  - About 25 percent of the site users are people over fifty.

The following disclaimer requirement by Christian Mingle was one of only a few sites asking users to **accept** terms about financial issues:

Important Notice: At Christian Mingle we want to protect you in your online dating experience, and we need your help to do so. Please read and accept this important message. I promise to never send money, ask others for money or share financial information with anyone I meet on Christian Mingle. In addition, I pledge to report anyone who asks me for money or my financial information.

Of course, this would only help with the guys/gals who play by the rules, and not those who prey on dating sites, so although this is a comforting statement, be aware of anyone asking or even mentioning money.

According to Wikipedia, ChristianMingle.com is owned by Sparks Networks, which also owns Elite Singles and Silver Singles among other dating sites. Sparks is the second largest dating owner in North America.

OurTime.com

Our Time is easy to join, a senior site with over 1.5 million users, and is one of the top senior sites for over-age-fifty seniors. One perk of Our Time is its ease of joining, and clearly it is designed for people who may lack fluency in the use of technology.

According to Wikipedia, OurTime.com is owned by IAC, People-Media, which is considered the largest dating site company in North America.

In our testing, as free users, Robert had over thirty "matches" in the first week. Gail had fifteen. The gender bias of this site is 55 percent of the users are women, and 45 percent are men. The geographic locations of the matches mostly fit into the two-hundred-mile criteria we set, and the age range of our matches generally fell between sixty-eight to seventy-eight years old. Our Time did not have a filter for widows/widowers, meaning we had both divorced and never-married people respond, and we had to sort them out. As stated in this chapter, we did not query any of the matches but reviewed their profiles and found they generally met our parameters of age and distance.

OurTime.com was easy to set up and get started—not as easy as Christian Mingle, but close. Our Time specifically says it does not check backgrounds, but like Christian Mingle, Our Time has a financial protection agreement that a user must actively approve.

Important Notice: To protect myself, I promise never to send money or share financial information with other Our Time users. In addition, I pledge to report anyone who asks me for money or my financial information.

As with other pledges, it is important to realize not everyone who signs the pledge is truthful.

According to ConsumerAffairs.com, some users complained they could not search for specific distances, but we did not find this to be the case. Our profile requests were generally met, but again we caution you to verify your information as you proceed. A user must sign up for a six-month minimum, about $100; however, they quote the charge as weekly, so the quoting shuffle strikes us as odd.

- **SITE NAME:** OurTime.com
- **PAID OR FREE:** Paid site with a limited free trial
- **AVERAGE SIGN-UP TIME:** > 5 minutes
- **PAID MEMBERSHIP PRICING:** Plans starting as low as $4.00 per week, minimum six months, but they also advertise $100 for a year.
- **UNIQUE OUR TIME FACTS AND FIGURES**
  - Forty-five percent of users are men and 55 percent are women.
  - Over 69 percent of users on Our Time identify as single parents.
  - One of the top ten fastest growing dating sites for singles age fifty plus.
  - Users can download a free IOS app, which has a four-star rating.

The Eight-Thousand-Site Question

Match.com

Match.com is one of the largest dating sites in North America with nearly eight million paid subscribers according to DatingAdvice.com. With this many users, the algorithm of matches is powerful, and Match.com does a good job of pairing up potential matches. Match has been in business for over twenty-five years.

Match.com, like OurTime.com, is owned by IAC, PeopleMedia, the largest dating site company in North America.

When signing up for Match.com, it is not as easy to set your dating preferences as Christian Mingle or Our Time, and thus Match rates as third as a senior dating site in our opinion. We found the choices in our selection senior-friendly, and the overall choices section seemed thorough, although completing the hour-long questionnaire consumed more time than we wanted to spend. They did not require us to complete it in order to have a free trial, but completing it yields better match opportunities.

Match.com also offers trips all around the world where you can meet other singles while having an adventure. Advertisements are often included in profiles. It also offers a video feature allowing interaction without sharing phone numbers.

In our testing as free users, Robert had over twenty-three "matches" in the first week, and Gail had thirty. This was different than our other experience, because the male match participation was greater than the female, which could be good news for the ladies! The gender bias of this site is 51 percent of the users are women, and 49 percent are men. The geographic locations of the matches lay generally within our two-hundred-mile criteria and fell within the sixty-eight to seventy-eight age range. We used the widow/widower preference, and we found our "matches" consistent with our requests with a few divorcees, indicating the function was useful, but not 100 percent.

Loving Again

While Match.com does not collect background information, it claims to have robust safety processes built in. Subscription fees start at the three-month base period. Match has been criticized about their auto-renewal policy, which allows them to roll you into the next payment period without your consent, so when you leave this dating site, verify you have canceled the auto-renewal feature and monitor your credit card account.

- **Site Name:** Match.com
- **Paid or Free:** Paid with limited free options
- **Average Sign-Up Time:** About 15 minutes
- **Paid Membership Pricing:** Plans starting at $15.99 per month, minimum subscription three months
- **Unique Match.com Facts**
    - Founded in 1995 and is headquartered in Dallas, Texas.
    - Match.com serves over fifty different countries.
    - The company is owned by Match Group, a company owning several online dating brands.

Match.com has a disclaimer similar to our other selections requiring the user to agree with a general safety statement in their terms and conditions:

We are not afraid to play it safe. In fact, we pride ourselves on it. From protecting your personal information to monitoring photos and profiles, Match is constantly working to maximize user safety.

Every user who creates a Match profile is expected to abide by and agree to our Community Guidelines. *Additionally, we offer in-depth* Safety Tips *to help you stay safe from the first message to meeting in person, and everything in between.*

You can improve the security of your account through phone number verification. It adds an extra layer of security to help protect your personal information.

The Eight-Thousand-Site Question

SilverSingles.com

Silver Singles is a site specifically for the over-fifty date-site user and is a popular dating site for seniors. They have been in business for seventeen years and have about half a million monthly users. According to HealthyFrameworks.com, Silver Singles is 100 percent dedicated to the age fifty and older dating consumers. They are a trustworthy and easy-to-use dating service proven to be successful for many seniors according to BestCompany.com. Silver Singles remains popular, but we found the sign-up time lengthy, nearly an hour, and thus we did not rank it as high as Match or Christian Mingle.

Silver Singles and their sister company Elite Singles are unique because they offer a personality test to their matching process. This test consists of 125 questions and seven essay-type questions. This personality test results in a five-factor sliding scale graph of openness, conscientiousness, extraversion, agreeableness, and neuroticism. The sign-up process is rather long because of this personality questionnaire, so be ready to spend at least an hour signing up for Silver Singles. However, it does yield a rather complete result with a basis for a scoring system for potential matches. The Silver Singles website algorithm matches the results of your personality test with your specific preferences to search their subscriber base and find the best possible matches for the user.

According to Wikipedia, Silver Singles is owned by Sparks Networks, which also owns Elite Singles and Christian Mingle among other dating sites, and Sparks is the second largest dating site owner in North America.

Silver Singles offers a coaching option. For an additional fee you can request help in writing your profile, and a dating profile writer will work with you to write a profile that may attract more "matches." This is available by phone if you prefer.

In our testing, as free users, Robert had over thirty-seven "matches" in the first ten days. Gail had thirty. Both had a good number of matches and a great response. The gender bias of this site is 59 percent women and 41 percent men, again reflecting the gender gap of aging of this group. The geographic locations of our matches fell within the two-hundred-mile criteria set, and the ages of our matches mostly met the sixty-eight to seventy-eight range. They used the widow/widower preference, and most matches fell into this category with only a few divorcees. As with other sites, check your preferred status.

- **SITE NAME**: SilverSingles.com
- **PAID OR FREE**: Both options available, limited capabilities with free membership
- **AVERAGE SIGN-UP TIME**: About one hour
- **PAID MEMBERSHIP PRICING**: Starting at $14.95 per month ($180 per year), with several different plans. Minimum subscription is three months. Shorter contracts seem to be less expensive, around $100 per year. Do the math!
- **UNIQUE FACTS AND FIGURES ABOUT THE SILVER SINGLES WEBSITE**:
  - The number-one rated app for seniors.
  - More than one-third of the members are fifty plus.
  - Get three to seven new matches daily.
  - Affordable membership options.
  - Professional help available for writing profile.

Silver Singles uses algorithm software for a safe environment, claiming to verify profiles daily to "keep the bad guys out." However, as with all dating sites, use your common sense as you contact these "matches" and potential life partners. Remember to stay within the Silver Singles app for the first week or so of communications, choose a neutral location for your FDA, and never share any financial information until you have complete confidence in him or her, and even then, take caution!

The Eight-Thousand-Site Question

According to BestCompany.com, all Silver Singles new member profiles are vetted by a special team to make sure they are valid and authentic. Members who are inactive on the site are automatically filtered out. Additionally, once your account has been set up, some things cannot be changed on your profile without contacting customer care, like your age, gender, name, and height. This encourages authenticity and honesty.

"Silver Singles offers these safety considerations:

1. Question unrealistic information.

2. Be mindful of your personal information.

3. Financial requests: If your partner suggestion requests for you to either make or receive any form of financial payment, cease all contact immediately and report the profile to customer care. This is one of the strongest indicators of a fraudulent account and it often only becomes apparent after initial contact has been made.

4. Don't rush, take your time.

5. Plan a safe meeting

- *Choose a neutral location, such as a coffee shop or a restaurant. Do not go to their house or invite them to yours for the first date.*
- *Tell your friends or someone you trust that you are going on a date and with whom.*
- *Do not drink too much alcohol.*
- *Do not leave your personal belongings unattended.*

6. Share your thoughts

In order to guarantee the authenticity of your recommended partners, we need your help. Email our customer care department with this form if you suspect any profile contains false information or is behaving in a fraudulent manner."

EliteSingles.com

Elite Singles describes itself as a dating app catering to singles who are more established in life and who generally have a higher education or career training. Eighty-five percent of the people who join Elite Singles claim to have some form of college education, university education, or higher-level training; however, we could not find any verification that these claims were true. Some reviewers commented that this site seems to be for more casual meeting than for long-term relationships. In our testing and review of profiles, we did not see this trend in our age group.

The age grouping of Elite Singles seems to be thirty to forty-five years of age, but has no shortage of quality matches, and nearly four hundred thousand new singles join every month according to Healthy-Framework.com.

Silver Singles and Elite Singles have many similarities because both use a personality test algorithm to match users and the personality tests are similar. The primary difference between the two is that Silver Singles is geared toward people over age fifty while Elite Singles markets itself to adults of all ages who hold at least a bachelor's degree and/or consider themselves professionals. Elite Singles and their sister company Silver Singles are unique from other sites in their use of a personality test in their matching process. Tests are nearly identical in content and length, with 125 questions and seven essay-type questions. This personality test results in five factors on a sliding scale graph of openness, conscientiousness, extraversion, agreeableness, and neuroticism.

The sign-up process for Elite Singles is rather long because you will spend nearly an hour in answering those personality questions and signing up. Both Silver and Elite Singles compare your answers to your "matches," resulting in a compatibility score that might help strengthen your matches. In personal experience, we found Elite Singles and Silver Singles shared a cross-over in their matches. For example, Robert joined

The Eight-Thousand-Site Question

Silver Singles but was contacted by people on Elite Singles, surprising both users.

In our testing, as free users, Robert had over forty "matches" in the first ten days, and Gail had twenty-five. The gender bias of this site is 56 percent of the users are women, and 44 percent are men. The geographic locations of our matches fell within the two-hundred-mile criteria set, and our matches fell within our requested age range. The widow/widower preference was used, and most matches fell into this category, with some divorce status showing up, which indicates the function was useful. But again, check for authenticity.

According to Wikipedia, Sparks Networks owns Elite Singles as well as Silver Singles and Christian Mingle among other dating sites, making Sparks the second largest dating site owner in North America.

- **Site Name:** EliteSingles.com
- **Paid or Free:** Paid, Limited Free Trial
- **Average Sign-Up Time:** Nearly one hour
- **Paid Membership Pricing:** Starting at $14.95 per month for a twelve-month subscription, or $180.00 for the annual contract. Shorter contracts are available and common, but you may have to search for this option.
- **Unique Elite Singles Facts and Figures:**
  - Nearly four hundred thousand new members monthly
  - Eighty-five percent of members hold an above average education.
  - More than 90 percent of members are over the age of thirty.

Elite Singles seeks to create a safe online dating environment for users. According to BestCompany.com, the dating app uses Profile verification, SSL Encryption, and a Fraud Detection System to protect private user information. These security measures help lower the risk of a user matching with a fake profile. However, Elite Singles recommends taking extra safety precautions when communicating with other members. If you suspect fraudulent behavior, you can report profiles to the customer care team.

eHarmony.com

eHarmony is a giant in sheer numbers, with over four million visits a month. Although they are not a senior-specific site, about 20 percent of the users on eHarmony are over age fifty according to DatingAdvice.com. Therefore, we rank them lower than some of the senior-specific sites. They are relatively easy to join, a little longer process than some, and use a compatibility quiz in their algorithm process to match users. They are on the expensive side, but the quality of matches is quite good. This site is for someone looking for something serious, but not a great site for a quick fling or something casual.

"I've become pretty intimately acquainted with eHarmony throughout this whole process. Overall, my eHarmony review revealed a dating site that might cost a few bucks extra, but in return you get results. If I had to do it all over again, eHarmony would be my first stop for a dating app for relationships and marriage."– *Jason Lee, Chief Editor of Best Online Dating*

The profile section is complete with written questions and a choice of prewritten answers selecting things you won't tolerate, and it allows you to ask questions of a potential match. We thought the profile process was good, although they stepped into the political arena a couple of times with questions about climate change and social activism, and we think sites should be agenda-free. eHarmony offers a free test-drive trial, a good thing while you are getting your feet wet.

In our testing, as free users, Robert had twelve "matches" in the first week. Gail also had twelve. eHarmony shows matches differently than

The Eight-Thousand-Site Question

some other sites, and you may not see large numbers like Christian Mingle or Our Time, but we found the matches met our profile questions with a high quality of matches, in our opinion. The gender bias of this site is 49 percent are women and 51 percent are men. The geographic locations and ages of our matches were compatible with our profile requests: two hundred miles and ages sixty-eight to seventy-eight. The widow/widower preference was used, and most matches fell in this category, indicating the function was useful, but check as you go.

- **Site Name:** eHarmony.com
- **Paid or Free:** Paid site with a limited free trial, occasional free communication weekends
- **Average Sign-Up Time:** 20-30 minutes
- **Paid Membership Pricing:** Plans start as low as $12.95 per month but entail a twenty-four-month contract or $310. Shorter contracts are available, but you may have to search for them.

Their safety statement is as follows:

Our Trust and Safety team works hard to ensure that you have the best possible experience. We routinely review accounts for inconsistent or suspect behavior. When communicating with or meeting a match, don't ignore your instincts. In any circumstance, your judgment and intuition are necessary to protect yourself.

- *Never give out your credit card number or bank account information.*
- *Never share your Social Security number, mother's maiden name or other private information like your address that can be used to access your financial information.*
- *Never send money or goods to a person.*

Always trust your judgment when you're on eHarmony. If you're feeling like a user has bad intentions, it's better to be safe and pause communication. Here's a list of common red flags when you're getting to know someone new:

- *Claims to be from the U.S. but is currently living, working or traveling abroad.*
- *Claims they are experiencing an emergency situation that requires your assistance, in either goods (i.e., computers or gift cards) or money.*
- *Disappears suddenly from the site then reappears under a different name.*
- *Wants the relationship to progress faster than you are comfortable going.*
- *Messages are poorly written and escalate quickly from introduction to a deeper connection.*
- *Asks inappropriate questions.*
- *Tells inconsistent or exaggerated stories.*
- *Gives vague answers to specific questions.*
- *Urges you to compromise your principles.*
- *Constantly blames others for troubles in his or her life.*
- *Insists on getting overly close, faster than you feel comfortable with.*
- *Claims to be recently widowed.*

FarmersOnly.com

FarmersOnly.com has emerged as a distinctive dating site because it is meant to be for farmers and ranchers living in rural areas and for those who share the values and interests of rural communities. It has four and a half million members and four hundred thousand users per month, which is low compared to the big boys. It is a basic site, easy to join and easy to understand. The selection process is whatever you say you are, matched with whoever you say you like, no matching algorithms, no psychological or personality test. While some people may be satisfied finding partners by using this niche dating site, others might have better luck using a dating site utilizing a matching algorithm to help users find a potential match.

Farmers Only was founded in 2005 by Jerry Miller, an agriculture salesman who saw a need for a social dating site for rural- and outdoor-oriented people. It has boomed into a niche market known for its quirky commercials and has become successful, attracting both men and women. With only a million farmers in the U.S., Farmers Only has over four times as many members. Farmers Only is not owned by a conglomerate.

If you consider yourself a part of, or longing for, the country folk lifestyle, FamersOnly.com may be a good place to find compatible, down-to-earth people. Farmers Only is all about filling this niche. Those who enjoy the outdoors-oriented, traditional farmer lifestyle and perceived values tend to report high satisfaction with the type of people they meet on the site. This dating site does not get much love from the big dating site reviews because, in our opinion, many reviewers are city folks. But if you're a city slicker, it doesn't mean you can't use this dating website.

In our testing, as free users, Robert had fifteen "matches" in the first week. Gail had twelve. The gender bias of this site is 61 percent of the users are women and 39 percent are men. This gender mix seems to beg the question, do women like this rural lifestyle more than men? The geographic locations of the matches mostly fell within our two-hundred-mile radius, and the ages of our matches generally met our age range. The widow/widower preference was not available, so the matches included divorced or single people, and the profiles do indicate marriage status, allowing a user to determine its importance.

Loving Again

Data about senior participation percentage of this site was not available. We found age matches in our testing and do not consider senior participation to be an issue, but it is not a senior-only site.

- **Site Name:** FarmersOnly.com
- **Paid or Free:** Free search available. Paid site includes benefits including upgrades
- **Average Sign-Up Time:** 10-20 minutes
- **Paid Membership Pricing:** Plans starting as low as $12.00 per month
- **Unique Farmers Only Facts and Figures:**
  - Over four million members.
  - Membership breakdown is 39 percent men and 61 percent women.
  - FarmerPhone allows you to receive and respond to platform messages through texting without login to your account (for an extra fee) which makes your computer time easier and shorter.
  - They have an automatic renewal, so be sure to cancel and monitor for charges if you leave the site.

Farmers Only offers basic safety features, such as allowing members to block other users. Any "catfish" schemes or scams result in the offending account being banned. However, Farmers Only does not conduct background checks on members, nor does the company require a strict verification process. In fact, FarmersOnly.com has no verification process. Users can create an account and browse other users' information without verifying who they are through social media accounts or email. A lack of safety features makes it easy for scammers or hackers to create fake profiles. Please use common sense and perhaps extra caution while using this site.

The Eight-Thousand-Site Question

Summary of Dating Sites

These dating sites are not the only ones available; there are over 8,000. We joined all the listed sites as generic persons and researched the sites for relevant data, reviews, or comments. Included in our ranking was the safety aspect, not only for financial protection but also regarding personal information and security.

We initially searched for those sites listed by Google, and cross-referenced the results, finding six of them listed in the top ten of the Googles sites. We then added FarmersOnly.com because it is an outlier and perhaps would give us an alternative result.

We found online dating reviews to lean toward the negative about many sites, but perhaps because it is easy for people online to sound off or maybe they perceived some real issues. Most of the negative comments mentioned price, difficulty of cancellation, or not being able to find the right person.

As we researched the actual dating sites, we became interested in what was happening with dating seniors. We encountered two surprises: first, that Internet dating was common in all age groups, from young people to seniors, and when we said we were dating, everyone had a story to tell. Second, as people told stories of meeting on the Internet, most negative stories mentioned exaggerated profile, misleading photos, or sites trying to upcharge or upgrade status. The one tragic story had to do with a rape of a young woman who, in meeting her match for the first time, got in his car and was abducted.

Almost all people said only good things, including stories of long-term relationships and marriages. So, good hunting but spend time to review and use your experience and common sense.

CHAPTER 13

WHAT A HUNK, BUT WHO IS THIS PERSON?

Hey! What eye candy! Loads of silver-haired vixens and foxes and, like a kid in a candy store, these mouthwatering choices are almost overwhelming. But before you swipe right to keep or left to delete, read the profile, again and again. What did they leave out? What are you attracted to? Are there immediate turn-offs or turn-ons?

∼ Gail's Story ∽

I was surprised, even shocked, to receive my first response. It was a heart from somebody I didn't know who lived about fifty miles from me. His picture looked okay, but before I could finish reading his profile, I had a few more photos of other potential daters pop up onto the screen. I wasn't sure what to do, so I did nothing, letting them float into my computer and stare back at me. I took my time and gazed at their pictures, wondering about their personalities and stories, whether they were good or evil and I read their profiles, some of which interested me, others not so much. Soon I had a mob of men, ages fifty to ninety, all excited to see me, and someone even asked me for a date. I said, "Slow down, Marine," to myself and shut down my computer. But the

What a Hunk, but Who is this Person?

next time I turned it on, I had a whole herd of men interested in talking to me, more than I ever dreamed. I had been a near dateless person in high school, college not much better, but look at this now! Holy cow, that many? I had decided to try out the adventure of online dating, but was I ready? Kinda like sheep in a holding pen, I needed to sort them out and select the ones who were keepers.

It is important to be discerning and select one or two, the best ones, the ones you have the most in common with, saving the rest for later (swipe right), just in case the first two fizzle. Handsome, good-looking people attract others, but you'll want to know who they are, where their lives have taken them, and what they want from a relationship. If you want an engaging conversation over a cup of coffee and the "match" wants something more, this might not be the person for you. Every person has a story, and knowing their story is important. Widowed? Divorced? Never married? Photos are nice, but the profiles tell the story, meaning you should read them, scrutinize them, fantasize about them, before making a lovely and logical choice. Some dating sites use a rating system when they "match" a couple. The systems are each a little different, but the basic rule is a higher score means they have a higher similarity to the profile you entered. Take notice of their system, but oh, by the way, did we mention to read and reread the profile? Look at the picture they posted and read between the lines, but read the profile.

If they sent you a "smile" or a "heart," and the profile seems right, take the next step and ask a question, something that doesn't matter. We used to ask, "What's your sign?" but you should update it for the 2000s with questions like "What's next on your travel list?" Or "What's your favorite Olympic event?" Or "Have you ever driven a hundred miles per hour?" Or "What was the last event or movie you saw?" Ask something that anyone can answer, but remember, their answer doesn't matter; its purpose is to start a conversation. If their answer gives you the willies, at least you've made a gesture. Chances are they will ask you something back, and you're off and running.

If you see a picture and profile you like, but the "match" hasn't responded, it's okay to respond with a smile or heart, but if you do, be prepared to receive something back. Remember, it's only a conversation starter, not a marriage proposal. The best conversation starters are open and honest comments, compliments, and humor, making him or her smile or laugh. Non-prying questions about work or favorite activities are good, and you should respond with upbeat answers, even humor. If your "match" asks you a prying question, be careful. And, as we have noted, questions and comments about finances and money are absolutely off-limits, and you should steer clear of them.

At this point, you will be texting within the dating site app, and your conversation should be relevant. You can make your texts flirty but not suggestive. It's okay for both of you to play a little hard-to-get. But if your "match" doesn't do anything for you, let him or her go; don't tease if you aren't serious.

Funny works well too, because everyone enjoys a bit of humor. Some sites offer you canned responses that you can simply "hit send," but you are better off to write from your heart or brain. If you have a favorite joke or one-liner, use it. Once.

The dating site's prewritten responses may sound like "love-bombing," trying to entice through gratuitous flirting. For example, on one site, Gail had a dozen or more potential daters tell her she had a great smile, using the exact words, "You have a great smile." The trouble was she wasn't smiling. She was riding an elephant and trying not to fall off. A natural comment would have been, "Where were you?" or "Do you always ride elephants?" But not one of them asked where she was or mentioned the elephant, only her great smile. The picture was from a trip in Thailand, bouncing through the jungle, and she had a great

What a Hunk, but Who is this Person?

story that would have made them laugh, but none of them gave her the chance to tell it.

We call this phase of the online adventure the start of intellectual intimacy, learning about someone, finding out who they are, figuring out if you could sit across a table at Starbucks or McDonald's and be able to carry on a conversation you would enjoy. We all have things we enjoy talking about as well as things that are off-limits. So, focus on the good things and shut down the off-limits.

Texting someone you don't know can be tricky, and it's easy to get off track. Our minds can run amok and get off subjects easily and quickly, and it might help to have some subjects in mind when you are texting for the first time, not like a job interview, rather reminding yourself of a recent trip or activity you particularly enjoyed. Texting is conversation and should be fun and flirty (but not provocative), and should demonstrate to your texting partner your communication style.

Generally speaking, drama is unwelcome and may be a deal breaker; after all, who wants to hear about your spouse's philandering ways or your brother's bout with gout? And, if you are texting several people simultaneously, try to keep them sorted out in your mind or take notes. For example, if you are talking to both George and Henry or Margie and Ruth, don't get the conversations confused, when one hates eggs for breakfast, but the other boasts about being a devoted Keto dieter. This book has a chapter called "Play-by-Play" to help you sort out the various conversations and keep track of your websites, passwords, and locations. This brings up the subject of how many people you are interested in, how much texting time you have, and whether to take it one at a time or have multiple text conversations, like sitting around the cafeteria table at the old high school with several dating prospects and flirting with them all.

Although you might be tempted to review your online match profiles daily, even several times a day, they can consume you, and checking only once or twice a week works well. Take your time to review profiles, photos, and responses.

❧ *Gail's Story* ❧

On our first online text, before I had a chance to ask where Robert lived, he texted three questions to me.

- *"Do you know how to swim?" What the heck did he mean? Were we going for a dip in a lake, or was he talking about the dating pool? I had taught swimming and been a lifeguard in my younger days and passed the Marine Corps swim test on the first try. I still enjoy going for a little swim in the summer. I said, "Sure, why? Do you have a swimming pool? I enjoy the water." He didn't answer but texted another question.*

- *"Do you have a passport?" Well, duh, I love travel and have been to a bunch of countries. I would drop everything to go on a trip tomorrow. "Why?" I repeated. I was now intrigued, but he didn't answer either of those questions.*

- *"Lastly, do you want to go to Paris?" Was this an invitation, a casual comment, or was he scamming me? I haven't been to Paris, somehow missed it on my various trips around the globe but would gladly go. I repeated cleverly, "Why?"*

At first, he didn't answer, which set my mind to racing, and he let me wonder what he was up to for nearly a day. Intriguing, but he still didn't answer. Swim. Passport. Paris. Did he want to swim to France? It was a long swim. Was he going to throw me off some raft and I'd be

What a Hunk, but Who is this Person?

on my own? Would he steal my passport and take some chickadee to Paris and leave me floundering in the Bermuda Triangle?

The next day he answered and stopped me cold with his text. "Paris is for lovers." Oh, my. I wasn't expecting that. His answer tugged at my heart, but I also enjoyed anticipating what he was going to say.

Among his questions, timing, and his final answer, I was hooked. It was romantic, no commitment, but I wanted to meet him. He was flirty, funny, and romantic. A winning trifecta.

❧ Robert's Story ❦

The first thing I look at as I open my "matches" is a picture, and if I don't like the picture (too blurry, no picture, too many people or pets, frowns, or someone looking like they have been laid out on a casket), I swipe left, tossing them into never-never land, knowing I will never see them again. Looking at a dozen profiles per site guarantees an hour or more of fun, looking at their photos, giving an icon of a flirty wink or smile to all who appeal to me, and swiping left when they don't. I can pretend I am Caesar Augustus at the Coliseum, deciding who lives and who dies. Swipe right to keep, swipe left to send to the lion's den. I can read their profiles, often fascinating, flirt a bit, which made me laugh as I hadn't flirted in a while, and select one or two lovelies who appeal to me. With a blind date, I get who I get, but online dating apps allow me to sort potential matches with no awkward silences or embarrassment and to choose the ones with the most potential.

If the photo pleases me, I read the profile, view other photos, and am selective about who I talk to, flirt with, or have visions of spending the rest of my life with (however long that might be). I find it fun to smile and laugh with these ladies, and we carry on, getting to know each other online, using the closed app within the dating site. No phone calls, no messaging, no visits, just texting online. We talk about our kids, our pets, and our past life, and in each case those conversations paint a picture of the writer on the other end of the website app. I don't know where they are, maybe a few miles from my home or farther across the country. Sometimes the conversations peter out; sometimes they start but then stop when one of us changes our mind, but if they don't, eventually we will agree to share phone numbers, leading to a phone call, FaceTime, or other video chat, and perhaps a little later, meeting at a mutually agreed neutral place for a cup of coffee or a meal. I never thought at my age anyone would be interested in me again, but here I am with more visitors than I can keep track of, causing me to buy a notebook to keep track of my suitors. Wow.

My life became interesting again. The sounds of silence faded and were replaced by thoughts of one or more certain mysterious ladies, mulling over our late-night texting and forming questions for the next texting session. I spent time evaluating the intellectual and emotional makeup of each lady, and my feelings of interest, wondering what she was really like. Would I see fireworks or an unlit match when we met? I knew of only one way to find out.

This process starts with writing texts, kind of like your grandma and grandpa did, courting with letters. When you join a dating site, you will write your profile and share your photograph and begin your risk management. You are on a closed text site, and no one can see your responses or comments except you and the other person, your "match." Remember: No personal data—such as your address, your email address, your phone number, your full name, and especially nothing about money, finances, or credit cards—should be shared. Now, you may think it is a silly thing to mention, but people get caught up in the excitement of love and romance and give out all kinds of risky information, including bank balances and account numbers.

What a Hunk, but Who is this Person?

Some use nicknames, which is okay, as long as they are accurate. Some people like to make up monikers, and Robert had some matches with names like "Doll Baby," "Princess," and "Lover Girl." Some of Gail's potential matches used names like "New Guy," "Mr. One and Only," "Handsome Dude." We wondered whether they were hiding something. Some might like these monikers, but they didn't appeal to us. Some matches used a shortened version, for example, using Ann for Annette or Joe for Joseph.

You should not base the choice of a match, through online dating or otherwise, on money. Money should not enter discussions during FDAs, casual conversations, or even heated discussions. Although the issue of money remains at the front of seniors' minds, it is inappropriate at this stage of your decision-making. Remember, if you are suspicious of someone trying to abscond with your well-cared-for retirement funds, your match is equally suspicious of you absconding with his or hers. Talking about money is a lose-lose conversation.

You begin to see winks and smiles from folks who want to talk with you. Some are "cool beans and hot horseradishes," but others you will ditch without giving them a second look. You can read the profiles, check all the posted photos, and if he or she doesn't appeal to you, you can move on by deleting the photo or swiping left (for many sites). If you like how he or she looks and how the profile reads, send a wink or a heart back.

Please remember good manners are good manners, always in style, and if you receive a smile or a wink, it's okay to take a risk and ask a question. Hearts and winks and thumbs-up can become commonplace or even misleading, so instead of an icon, send words. You might ask a question suited to the profile they have posted. Start the conversation with a question, like "I see you like to travel. Where is your favorite place?" or "Maps or books? Which do you prefer?" and the conversation should continue.

Continue the texting within the dating site's app. While most people enjoy a sense of humor and cleverness, it is also important to be normal, interesting, and above all, truthful, talking about adventures and dreams. One-word answers like "yes," "no," "maybe," are conversation stoppers; use your imagination and remember you are texting—many times texts will pass each other and land out of order, leaving you uncertain of where you are in the conversation, but you will be able to enjoy the rhythm of the chat.

Texting to a match within an app, although it might be awkward, safeguards your personal information, a safety feature built into dating apps. No one can trace your fingerprints or find your phone number if you stay within the dating app. We cannot say this strongly enough. For those of us who worry about safety and the Internet, this is important.

Your objective during this pre-date period is to find out if this match will work based on the relatively little information you have. The texting process inside the dating site app protects you. You have given nothing up as to your identity, including location, phone number, email, or your last name. You will want to continue texting within the app until you feel confident about sharing your phone number, which would allow you to text using your phone number. This is called going live, or IRL, *In Real Life*, but you should not go live on the spur of the moment. Rather, think about it, sleep on it, and be certain.

Reaching out by phone or email is the first step in gaining trust of each other, and our experience suggests you should text about twenty to fifty or more messages for at least a week within the dating site app before sharing your phone number. Continue to text only until you feel confident enough to be ready for a phone call. Remember, once you share one phone number, your identity opens to your match. After sharing phone calls—and again, several texting sessions would not be too many—the next normal event is to meet. When one of you says, "I

What a Hunk, but Who is this Person?

really want to meet you," and the other replies, "Sounds good. What is a nice neutral ground?" it will be time to take the meet-and-greet plunge. Of course, tell your friends and family you are meeting your "match," also telling them the name of the site and time and your expected return. If, for some reason, the time and site are changed, cancel the meeting and keep your friends and family informed.

We both remember: *This old seventy-six-year-old heart is so excited that I can't stand it, a real date! I spend an hour in the bathroom, showering until my skin is red. I look at this old body in the mirror, wondering what he or she will see in me, but, by golly, it is time to hitch up these fancy duds, splash on some sweet-smelling stuff, and strut out the door to begin this grand adventure.*

CHAPTER 14

THE FIRST DATE ADVENTURE

"Do you want to meet for coffee?"
"Yes!" he texted back when she asked.

❧ *Robert's Story* ❧

I recall that I couldn't stop smiling. I'd liked everything we had talked about, and I wanted to make a good first impression, and I hoped she was everything that I thought she was. I girded and preened like a bullfighter with Bolero playing in the background, visions of bikini-clad Bo Derek romping through my seventy-seven-year-old mind. I put on my best pair of starched Wranglers, my best dress shirt, my new boots, and another shot of cologne and headed out the door. Who knows? This could be the beginning of a great adventure.

For the first time since losing Patty, I started looking for another woman in my life, and boy, I found all kinds of choices whom I had never seen before, eye candy, all sizes and shapes with great profiles. Later I learned some profiles stretched the truth, perhaps wishful thinking on the part of the author. When I learned of the insincerity, I changed my profile to read, "No lies, no drama." A lie will haunt a future relationship, and you may get your foot in the door, but it can get you kicked right out the same door. Untruthfulness, embellishment, exaggeration,

The First Date Adventure

and gaps in the truth are some of the risks of online dating. A lie about something insignificant means bigger lies may be coming, and where do you draw the line? Drama is the same. When I read the text or listened to a phone call that emphasized the tragedy of past life, it struck me as "poor me," making me wonder if she saw drama in everyday life or if she had not resolved the issues of her lost partner. I have faced enough tragedy for a lifetime and don't want to engage in more. This would be something like relating the tragedies heard in country-western songs, my dog dying, my house burning down, and losing my glasses, all in the same day. No one is interested in those tragedies, especially when online dating.

The mating dance gave me the chance to flirt with some really interesting ladies. I could read their profiles, look at the photos, and be selective about whom I might convince to spend the rest of my life with. It was fun, I smiled and laughed with these ladies, we flirted, we talked about our kids, our pets, and our past life, and in each case those conversations painted a picture of the lady writer. Sometimes it petered out, sometimes it started and stopped, and sometimes we met at a neutral place and had a coffee or a meal. Finally, I had something to look forward to. I spent time evaluating the intellectual and emotional makeup of the lady, my feelings of interest, and how to determine whether she was "right" for me. Was she shy or just modest? Was she outgoing or bossy, and was she as curious about me as I was about her?

After we had texted within the app and all looked well, we shared phone numbers and chatted within our phone numbers and had some conversations, including a video phone chat, which solidified that first date.

LOVING AGAIN

❧ *Gail's Story* ❧

Gail recalls thinking: He is six hundred miles away on a combine in the middle of a barley field in Montana, and we've been texting nonstop for days, and he intrigues me. I thought to myself, it is time for a little less talk and a lot more action, so I said it: "Let's meet." He answered, "Yes, good idea." What was I thinking? My Marine Corps stubbornness wouldn't let me back out, meaning I had to go to the store because I had no dating clothes and no perfume, among other things. My hair was a mess, and my last lipstick had melted in the sun. So off to Dillard's I went to get my preening supplies and new duds. We each had to travel 307 miles to meet, so we set a date, and I took a deep breath, closed my eyes, and wondered what my kids would say.

My online dating experience was more limited than Robert's, as I had joined only one dating site, a free one on Facebook. I was looking for basic information about going online to meet and greet someone new, to dance with a new partner, so to speak, to increase my knowledge, to find out what I had to do, and planned to stay on it for only a few days. Initially, Robert sent me a flirty text, which I answered, and we enjoyed a few evenings of texting on the app before moving to having phone conversations, eventually video chats. Sometime during these phone conversations, I finished my research and cancelled my free subscription, although Robert and I continued to talk. Facebook didn't realize I had cancelled, and I had several weeks of Facebook messages saying, "Tim wants to meet you," or "Look at Wayne, he's waiting." A few weeks later, the app seemed to disappear from Facebook, and my long list of lover boys disappeared as well. In my limited experience, I was glad I met Robert, and, as soon as we met, a lot of sparks began flying like lightning bugs on a dark night's sky.

The First Date Adventure

What I learned from being on this dating site was that I was not specific enough in my profile. I had failed to think through the kind of person I was looking for, but remember, I was researching for a book, so it didn't matter. I determined faith and political party were important, although not critical. I had taught English for many years and decided the ability to write a clear and coherent sentence with proper punctuation would rate high. Otherwise, I found myself correcting his comments, in red, like schoolteachers do. Location wasn't important but should have been. Robert and I lived about six hundred miles apart, making it difficult to get together for quick visits, although we had a standing nightly date on the phone, often lasting two or more hours. I learned I needed to have questions ready to go, which I hadn't thought about. I never lie, but was tempted, because sometimes lies would have made my story better or easier to tell. (Remember, I write fiction.) Robert doesn't like drama and neither do I, but our definitions of drama were not always the same, so it was absent from our visits and phone calls. Most of our conversations dealt with the present and the future because the past is past.

In my Marine Corps training, I learned to watch for danger, and of course, I implemented those safeguards into my online dating adventures.

Advice: Meet in a public place: Your first date shouldn't be a movie night in your home. If you're ready to meet someone in person, do it in public. A restaurant or coffee shop might be a good choice. You shouldn't give out your address until you've established a trusted relationship. Men, let the women make the choice. This is not a hard-and-fast rule, but remember, allowing the vulnerable partner to pick the mutual spot is like opening the car door or helping them on with their coat; it is just good manners. Women, absolutely pick the place where you will be comfortable. If he disagrees, think twice. In our intermountain region, a bar is usually a restaurant, so don't judge too harshly if she says, let's meet at the Mint, or the Interlude, or the Shamrock.

ADVICE: TRUST YOUR GUT. If something feels off, trust your vibes. Some people worry about being rude and ignore their gut feeling that something is wrong. Good manners are important, but safety trumps good manners.

ADVICE: DON'T DRINK A PREORDERED DRINK. If you arrive at a bar or restaurant for a date and a drink sits on the table waiting for you, it's a red flag. To be on the safe side, order your own drinks and watch them being delivered. Depending on your cultural background, it's not a bad idea to pay for your own drinks.

ADVICE: HAVE A BAILOUT PLAN. If you go on a date, let a friend know where you are and when you plan to return. Plus, create a code word with a friend as an escape plan. For example, if you text your friend, "Having a great time," it means she should call you immediately with an "emergency," forcing you to leave or even drop by the restaurant, interrupting your date. This plan works for a variety of dating problems, from a boring date to a scary one. Some people even turn phone location apps on so friends can track their whereabouts, as an additional safety precaution.

ADVICE: DRIVE SEPARATELY. During an initial get-to-know-you phase, you should *always* drive separately. Getting into a stranger's car comes with risks, so drive to and from that first date in your own car. If you decide to make multiple stops, like from a restaurant to the movie theater, drive separately. Riding together should wait until you both have established trust in the relationship, and only you know what trust feels like.

ADVICE: BE PREPARED. If talking to a stranger frightens you, prepare yourself. Compile a small list of things you could talk about, anything and everything from school to ancestry to grandkids to your favorite movie or dinner. Then, leave the list at home, and be confident that you

The First Date Adventure

can move forward with stories or adventures that will charm the heck out of him or her.

We discovered in our texting and later our phone calls a growing interest in the other person. The interest was sparked by words or phrases that led to more things to talk about. Our common subjects appeared to be inexhaustible, and perhaps the most interesting thing we both discovered was the lure of adventure. We found we were curious about the world around us, whether in Africa or just down the street. Both of us are well read, so when one of us mentioned Casablanca, Maracaibo, or Nome, Alaska, we already knew something about it, regardless of whether we had seen it in person. Our conversations led us in different directions from where they started. For example, one night we talked about growing and harvesting malt barley for Coors in Montana and then picking strawberries in an Idaho field, which reminded us about our common agricultural roots, then led to some of the cities we had visited and the sights we had seen around the world. Those led to our mutual interest in boats, Gail's large, with cruise staff and a handsome Norwegian captain and elegant dinners, Robert's with his grandkids serving as crew on a much smaller vessel, exploring the rivers of North America, eating peanut butter and jelly sandwiches.

The point of our conversation was to become more intimate intellectually so we could listen to each other and talk, and it brought a smile to our souls. We found ourselves sharing things no one knew, even our former spouses, increasing our vulnerability and opening ourselves to the possibility of a strong relationship. This intellectual intimacy bonded us closer and closer until in some conversations we seemed to be one person, not two.

The First Date, the FDA

One of the two of you says, "Let's meet!" and the other one says "Yahoo!" and you agree on a site you both know or know of, a neutral site, perhaps halfway between your houses. It could be in the same city, at a coffee shop or a fancy restaurant. You agree on a time, discuss details like parking, how you will recognize each other, who pays, and you are off!

LADIES: Dress for success, not your sequined dress, but not sweats and a T-shirt, either something comfortable but stylish. Think of Ingrid Bergman when she returned to see Rick in *Casablanca*. She was all woman and she meant business. Repeat after me slowly and with feeling, "Oh, Rick." You've got one shot at this. If he's Mr. Right, don't mess it up! And you can't go wrong with a pearl necklace or a gold chain.

GENTLEMEN: Take a bath, shave or trim, dress like this is the most important date in your life, because it could be. A man should never have regrets about how he looks in front of his new lady. Remember *Cat Ballou*, the movie with Lee Marvin and his girdle he put on before the gunfight. Play "Bolero" while dressing, and remember, a little "Old Spice" goes a long way.

The date is on. Look her in the eye, smile, give a friendly hug, and walk to your table. Don't look at your watch, not even once!

CHAPTER 15

SLOW DANCE, ROMANCE

Romance! It can be about flowers and chocolates, but mostly with flirting, laughing, teasing, and expressed longing, it is a shared emotion in a more intimate way than an informal relationship.

Romance is the logical second stage of a relationship, if anything can be logical about love. The thrill of a new conversation, the longing for those flirtatious words, the excitement of a touch or kiss, all are a part of this primordial soup of emotion and joy that is built into our DNA. We become as giddy as teenagers, losing our train of thought, leaving common sense behind for this newfound passion. And wow, does it feel great!

There is romantic magic in flowers or negligees or cards on special days like Valentine's Day or on a birthday, but also the magic of romance arrives on a plain old Wednesday, when you are half sick with a cold, dog-tired from a rough day at work, or you have simply had a bad day, and someone brings you flowers or kisses you unexpectedly on the neck. Romance means the most during those times, for no reason at all.

We all love romance. We adore having someone special pay attention to us, demonstrate affection, desire, and getting those juices flowing. Humans, by nature, are social animals and crave interaction with others, and when done by that special person with thoughtfulness and gentleness, it touches the soul.

Romance can appear in many forms. Flirting is a natural part of romance, giving us the chance for easy communication as we sort out the words of that special person who made us laugh or even blush. We all have our own style, and none of us are alike; we notice and enjoy things differently, we express ourselves as one individual to another, so the rules of romance are hard to pin down. In the library you can easily find *The Hitchhiker's Guide to the Universe*, but a universal guide to romance for a special person lies only within our own minds. Famous authors from Shakespeare to F. Scott Fitzgerald have told romantic classics that we know, but it is difficult to get a handle on this slippery subject. We understand romance, we feel the inner warmth and glow of feeling a special person's attention, but having a guide affirming that one thing is romantic and another not, well, this is almost impossible.

One of the main paths to romance is simple: paying attention to what he or she says. If he says, in an offhanded manner, "Man, I hate corned beef cabbage," then a different dish might be appropriate on St. Paddy's Day, or if she says, "Candles are a waste of money," think twice before you buy perfumed candles for your romantic Valentine's Day dinner. But these are silly rules. Your heart dictates the right moves; sometimes they are right, other times they are wrong. If these moves fail, then maybe it wasn't meant to be. You should not change yourself to fit someone else's idea of romance. Some men would never be caught dead in a fancy department store's negligee section, while some women would race to a farm supply store to buy men's cologne.

Romance is baked into our psyche, yet over time we take it for granted and forget how important romance can be to our significant other. We become tired or bored or distracted and ignore the needs of our partner, and suddenly it's too late. When he or she dies, we think,

Slow Dance, Romance

If only I had...? We fill in the blank and feel regret for what we didn't do, those last few days, weeks, months, or even years. But now is the time to make up for those forgotten romantic gestures. And, let's be honest, they are fun and seductive, make you smile, laugh, giggle, and even blush, and that is a good thing.

Romance is indefinable, but as Supreme Court Justice Potter Stewart so eloquently said of obscenity in *Jacobellis v. Ohio* in 1964, "I know it when I see it." We, too, recognize romance when we see it or feel it or are moved by it. Romance comes easily to some, while others stumble with it. It looks different from what we envisioned in high school, or when we watch Netflix or read romance novels. Being romantic is no different from years ago when we met our spouses on the sock hop floor with big corsages, to today's texting of a beautiful poem just for her, or a quiet moonlit dinner for two on a romantic dinner cruise.

Romantic adventures can occur in the most abstract ways, the early morning toothpaste kiss, holding the door for your partner, a candlelit dinner when you are having grilled ham and cheese, a flower from the garden, turning off the TV and dancing to a golden oldie, and, of course, pillow talk. Or how about a regular Friday night date, or even better, a surprise date, going out for a pizza or a view of the mountains. None of these suggestions cost much money, but they will remind you and your partner that this bond is important and cherished, the essence of romance and adventure.

An adventure isn't complete without laughter, and we have found that our best memories come from the humor of an event. Laughter is the food of the soul, the appetizer, the main course, and dessert. People say love makes the world go around, but laughter is equally important. Widows and widowers, almost without exception, have been deprived of laughter for a while, and it can wear us down without realizing it. A quiet giggle, a chuckle, or an inward snicker can brighten our moment, but a robust belly laugh will enliven our week. You know we are right. Eskimos call making love "laughing together," which seems appropriate.

❧ *Gail's Story* ❦

The first time Robert made me laugh, he and I had not yet met and were talking on the phone, and I let out a raucous belly laugh at something he said. He had made some stupid comment or asked a stupid question, as men in my life often do, and it struck me as funny. All of a sudden, my life changed. I knew what I was missing. I looked around the kitchen to see where the noise had come from and realized I was the only person in the room. I enjoyed the humor and became hungry for it. I had passed through enough sadness and grief to last a lifetime and decided I enjoyed laughing a whole lot more than the silence that had plagued me for nearly four years. I recalled laughing a few times at my grandchildren's attempts at jokes, including my granddaughter's obsession with SIRI, the phone voice, telling me jokes so corny that they often fell flat. I chuckled at the playfulness of dogs and the absurdity of some television shows, and writing Wrinkly Bits stories about senior citizens falling in love seems a funny enough concept. The problem was that I had laughed alone, giggling to myself about the words that flowed from my fingers. I came to realize that laughter is also a communal thing. To achieve the full benefit of laughing, we must laugh with someone. Another person must join into our levity, because half of a joke or funny event is how another person responds.

I've never really thought of myself as a humorous person—can't tell a joke to save my soul, or anyone else's either, and often forget a punchline—yet lots of people laugh at my writing and comments. I thought this strange until I realized that laughter is rarely linked with humor. Whew. Laughter, for me, is often situational, the wrong thing happening at the wrong time, the wrong thing turning out right, and the right thing turning out wrong, and examples live all over the place, such as the cowboy loving both airplanes and cows but hanging out with a city girl. What the heck?

❧ Robert's Story ❧

My attempts at romance on my first two or three online matches frustrated me, which might have been meant to be. I told Match No.1, "I like to go to the movies," and she told me, "You can buy them on TV. Why waste your money?" Then, another turndown, after ordering a juicy T-bone, she remarked, "I see you are a rancher, but cows are environmentally harmful," and boy, did that take the wind out of my sails. Those dates went nowhere as did my romantic thoughts. Gail, on the other hand, understood my corny jokes and teasing and could give as good as she could take. Our vocabularies, interests, and love of adventure matched, and we discovered that we laughed at the same things. This romance grew and blossomed. When she puts her hands on her hips and sticks her jaw out, saying, "What are you talking about this time, Cowboy?" it cracks me up every time. Even thinking about it, I smile.

Many people and agencies have engaged in studies of humor and have found it helps keep people healthy in a variety of ways, physiologically and psychologically. Humor keeps your mind sharp, but it helps physical health as well. The studies have found humor has positive effects on everything from heart health to cancer to pain tolerance to stress to rheumatoid arthritis. It even lessens some of the symptoms of Parkinson's disease, one of the more difficult diseases to diagnose and cure. And what can be more fun than laughing? Dr. Patch Adams' *Gesundheit Institute* saw the health benefits of laughter and encouraged hospitals to use humor and laughter as therapy. Now many hospitals have clown units and involve laughter as a part of their healing processes. Laughter Yoga, which trains people to laugh, is available in many places.

Since we began laughing again, we have found it easier and easier to see the humor in our lives, which helps us to be optimistic and adventurous. Even the concept of online dating seems funny. Who would think a nerdy twenty-year-old could write a computer program to help us highly sophisticated and experienced senior citizens find romance and maybe love? It makes us giggle when we run across some weird twenty-something slang in a senior website. He or she might know how to write code, but for heaven's sake, what does a twenty-something know about love, especially love after retirement?

Emotional intimacy is that exciting feeling of falling in love. It is the quickening of the heart when your love is near, and the laughing at jokes only the two of you understand. It is the feeling of being safe with each other, the ability to talk about things, intimate things that you may never have thought about, varying from why our grandkids stare at small black cubes as they sit next to each other, to why are we here, why does God allow terrible things to occur, and what toothpaste we prefer. We laugh, we cry, and we share. We build on our intellectual intimacy by understanding the other person's beliefs, their wants, and their needs. With this sharing, we merge our lives and, indeed, our souls together. This interaction increases intimacy, both intellectually and emotionally, and leads us into further romantic adventures that banish the misery of silence. Romance is the spice that we all need, and it flavors this delicious mix with laughter, kisses, and the gentle thoughts of love. Our lives only get better with a whiff of perfume or cologne, a smile, and the lure of romance.

CHAPTER 16

SEX: Now that I've Captured Your Attention

Now that you've met your dating match, you'll be reminded that the excitement of thinking about sex with someone you love is one of the most wonderful feelings in the world. We have known love, felt it, and then lost it, and here we go again. As widows and widowers, this ultimate intimacy excites and frightens us at the same time. As Hunter S. Thompson so wisely says, "Sex without love is just as bad as love without sex." So here we old people are, in love and liking it. Where do we go from here?

Usually when we talk about intimacy, we think of sex, which, of course, is one huge component of a relationship and perhaps the best, but at our stage of life, we enjoy the adventure of all the senses, seeing the physical person as desirable, the sight, the sound, the smell, the taste, and the feeling of being touched by this caring person with whom we have established an intellectual and emotional intimacy bond.

❧ *Robert's Story* ❧

In the beginning of my online adventure, I looked at many photographs of women on the various websites, some eye candy and some not, and I made almost instantaneous choices to flip to the left (delete) or right (keep) depending on my preferences and unconscious desires. I don't know any particular trait that makes a woman appeal to me or not, and wonder if it is influenced by my mother, the movies, or Playboy magazines of my youth. Bo Derek, frolicking on the beach with Ravel's "Bolero" playing in the movie 10 was my ideal in the seventies, but now in my seventies, my lady and I enjoy a hot tub soak with "Unchained Melody" playing, fantasizing about what might or might not happen later. I know what I really like in a silver-haired vixen: a classic lady, my age, with curves, a nice smile, and pretty eyes. Not skinny and not fat, but curvy.

I was lucky. I met Gail through her online picture standing next to a lock, through her profile, and with her texts. We moved right along to a date where we touched and gazed into each other's eyes, and I could finally say, "Wahoo." I could see her, smell her, touch her hand, listen to her laugh, and imagine spending more time with her.

As we traveled down this trail of pictures and profiles, first texting, then phoning, and finally dating, we established intellectual and emotional intimacies. We shared our life stories, the causes of our happiness and laughter, as well as our grief and tears, and found we shared many common paths. The romance was thrilling, exciting even. What was next? As we have grown closer with our minds and our hearts, we savor the touch of the hand, the excitement of a shared kiss, and the tingle of our lower forty when we embrace while saying, "Hello," or "Good night, my darling." All these are important to build the trust, and as time passes, we both long for more. We are no longer teenagers grappling in the back seat with those infernal bra straps and impossible positions as we tried to figure out how to satisfy ourselves. Our life experiences of been-there-done-that have taught us what we like and, more importantly, what our partner may like.

SEX: Now that I've Captured Your Attention

The largest sex organ is our brain, according to Erica Jung, the feminist author of Fear of Flying *and now author of* Fear of Dying. *I read Ms. Jung in 1973 in my quest to understand the women of my time, but I am still in the dark as far as women are concerned. As General Patton famously said about Rommel, "You glorious bastard, I read your book," as he defeated the German tanks in north Africa. I said of Erica Jung, "You glorious feminist, I read your book," and it helped me understand those glorious ladies of the 1970s. At my age I am still mystified about the silver-haired versions of these gals, but the thrill, romance, and mystique make every day and night worth living.*

While they look different from those lovelies of the seventies, those in the seventies are far more appealing. They have opinions based on years of experience, wisdom from what they have learned, good manners, and are fully capable of knowing about building an enduring relationship.

The question of sex for widows and widowers of our age has been researched. The evidence strongly suggests many of us remain sexually active, and sexual relations are healthy for us. And, not only healthy, but because we know what we like, they are satisfying.

Loren Stein of the National Council on Aging reporting in "The Seventy-Year Itch" found half of seniors, ages sixty or over, have sex at least once a month, and an equal number want to have sex more frequently. Another finding: "People find their mates more physically attractive over time." Similarly, AARP reports two-thirds of their respondents said sex interested them, and more than 40 percent of Americans ages sixty-five to eighty admit to being sexually active, according to their 2018 survey.

Along with pleasure, seniors may be medically benefiting from sex: a stronger immune system, improved cognitive function, cardiovascular health in women, and lower odds of prostate cancer in men. As we have noted, negative thoughts and loneliness lead to several health maladies in seniors, including dementia and Alzheimer's, and by allowing the relationship to grow through the sexual experience, the excitement of what may come and the thrill of bare skin on bare skin pushes those negative thoughts back into the folds of your brain. And research, as well as common sense, suggests sex improves sleep patterns, reduces stress, and cultivates intimacy.

Researchers throughout the world confirm that sex leads to better cognitive functioning in older folks, protecting people from memory loss and other cognitive impairments. Multiple studies have shown older men and women who are sexually active enjoy increased levels of general cognitive function. These effects may be due to the action of hormones such as testosterone and oxytocin, which are influenced by sexual intercourse. We found multiple studies confirming consensual sex was healthy and none indicating the opposite. Mood, memory, and general health all seemed to be improved because of sexual activity. So, next time you're about to slip between the sheets with your special someone, just remember that this moment of passion will spark a whole neural firework show, releasing a special hormonal cocktail that will, at its best, charge a whole set of biological batteries.

"Use it or lose it," says geriatrics expert Walter M. Bortz, author of three books on healthy aging as well as several studies on seniors' sexuality. Dr. Bortz, a professor at Stanford Medical School, is past president of the American Geriatrics Society and former co-chair of the American Medical Association's Task Force on Aging. "If you stay interested, stay healthy, stay off medications, and have a good mate, then you can have good sex all the way to the end of life," he says. A Duke University study shows some 20 percent of people over age sixty-five have sex lives better than ever before, he adds.

In 2005, Peggy J. Kleinplatz, a University of Ottawa professor and sex researcher, began interviewing people with active sex lives. Previously, sex research focused on dysfunctional marriages and relationships, but she began looking at what makes a deeply fulfilling sexual relationship. She found rich sexual relationships were possible, regardless of health, age, and socioeconomic status. Her 2020 book, *Magnificent Sex: Lessons From Extraordinary Lovers*, with co-author A. Dana Ménard, is based on research involving relationships considered to be good, as opposed to the bad and ugly. Forty percent of the participants were older than sixty. "Who better to interview about fulfilling sex than people who have practiced it the longest?" Kleinplatz said. She also noted some of these "extraordinary lovers" revealed upon entering middle age, their forties and fifties, they realized they had set their expectations for sex too low. If they wanted significantly better sex, they knew it required a commitment of energy and effort. "It takes so much willingness and courage to show yourself naked, literally and metaphorically," Dr. Kleinplatz says.

In other words, as we age, we understand how much better sex can be, and if we are an extraordinary lover, we will spend the mental effort and energy needed to open our minds and allow vulnerability and honesty into our lovemaking. The intellectual side of our brain begins to mesh with the human animal side to bring conscious actions—like saying, "I really like it when you do that" or "Touch me gently here"—and more communication into our lovemaking. Because the brain is the largest sex organ in our body, as we get older, our brain becomes more important with a strong primal urge. Passion, after all, is romance, but our brain tempers our passion in wanting to please our partner, and we consciously stay a little longer in this special place.

The brain is the center of our pleasure control, and if we want our partner to fully join in the fun and enter the realm of extraordinary lovers, we must communicate. We like pillow talk, just the two of us, in our special, safe space, surrounded by the thoughts and smells of our lover. We pillow talk each night before we go to sleep, and it is intimate, intellectually, emotionally, and sometimes sexually. We laugh and talk, first about what went on in our day, maybe the grandkids, and gradually shift topics to us, how we feel, what adventures still lie ahead, what we want from life and from this night.

It is important to tell your partner, in those tender moments, what she does to make you feel like a man and what you can do to make her feel more like a woman and her moments more enjoyable. Opening up to another person can be scary, but if you want fulfillment, be brave, open up, and ask for the same. By this time, you may have set boundaries—oral sex, anal sex, sex toys—which should be agreed upon and talked about. Be light and humorous, not setting a rigid rule, but as a guide, "I may not like that, but I really, really like this." Laugh, cuddle, and allow the conversation to move toward "let me show you" and "do you like this?"

Of course, we remember our backseat gymnastics during our teenage years. Now seventy plus, with the minds and emotions still full of vim and vigor, but less agile bodies, we creak in places too numerous to mention. Some positions are impossible, but what the heck, trying is so fun, and orthopedic surgeons are readily available (and need to earn a living), so talk and laugh about it. However, tree positions in the shower add danger for us, and if we fall, the ambulance drivers will not be thrilled about untangling these old, wrinkled bodies. And then what do you tell your kids while in traction in the hospital? As I heard long ago, "It wasn't a particularly special ride, but you do have a cute way of getting off and on." I never knew what she meant, but I took any compliment I could get. In these days, my style is a bit more measured, and I always keep in mind the difficulty of explaining to an ambulance driver how I ended up under the bed with a dislocated shoulder or twisted knee, naked as the day I was born.

As wise old seniors, instead of the backseat romp, we will get two rooms adjoining at a grand hotel with a spa and a great breakfast. We enjoy the lovemaking as a shared gift and as an adventure, laughing into our pillows as we spend our romantic nights loving amidst a bed-scape of tangled sheets and shared bliss.

❧ *Gail's Story* ❦

Robert told me I had to write the chapter about sexual intimacy. So, I'm well over seventy and know what sexual intimacy is, but how do I write a chapter about it? Here goes nothing, but don't tell my kids.

For those of us who are senior citizens, especially over the age of seventy, the words "sexual intimacy" can strike fear and panic deep into our soul. As teenagers, then young adults, middle-aged adults, and even old adults, we tossed the word "sex" around like a big pizza pie. No big deal. Even so, we kept details about our sexual activity to ourselves and our partner, but we didn't really try to hide anything. Being widowed, I had not had sex for a while, I can't even remember how long, and now it is a big deal. My friend said, "I'm not ready to sleep with just anybody. I loved my husband, and he was enough for me for eternity." Another friend, male, told me, "I'm afraid of STDs. Some women are promiscuous, and they might give me something, so I'm not having sex. It's all over the news. It's too dangerous."

Describing sexual intimacy is difficult for me, but the old descriptor of being "turned on," even in my seventies, is real. My lower forty grumbles and growls in the most pleasant of ways, and all five senses come into play. I can smell, taste, see, and feel what's happening to me. I'm deaf as a post, so won't add the hearing thing. Years ago, the Righteous Brothers sang a song called "Unchained Melody," which has the words "I hunger for your touch," and oh, man, is that ever true.

These friends who don't want sexual intimacy are both right and wrong. Molly Kavanaugh of "Kendal at Oberlin," a blog site, identified four myths about sexual activity in the aging process and published a report entitled, "The Myths About Sexuality and Aging."

"**MYTH 1:** You can do nothing about normal body changes that interfere with sexual activity and enjoyment."

The fact is that we now have plenty of treatments, supplements, and medicine for erectile dysfunction in men and dryness in women. Ask your doctor. He or she should answer your questions, and it will give them something fun to think about when the day is over. And the drugstore clerk's eyes will pop out of her head when you ask where you can find vaginal lubricant and buy two bottles, extra-large. It's worth the price of admission, just thinking about it.

"**MYTH 2:** Sex causes heart attacks."

The truth is, not a chance, it is good exercise, but check with your doctor if you have doubts. Shoveling snow is much more apt to cause a heart attack, and having sex is a whole lot more fun. Think of that when your lover tells you to shovel the sidewalk; just turn to her and say, "The doctor says that sex is safer. How about a little romp?"

"**MYTH 3:** Sex isn't important when you get older."

Oops, wrong again. Sexual health and intimacy are important no matter how old you are; in fact, since loneliness is such an important factor in seniors' health, the touching and caring help to remove the loneliness and promote well-being. Just the touch of another person on your shoulder or some other body part can arouse or distract you from the task at hand.

"**MYTH 4:** Older adults don't have to worry about sexually transmitted diseases."

False! The truth is quite the opposite, and the fault lies with those of us who are in our seventies. Read on.

In the 1960s and '70s, in the middle of the sexual revolution, which we baby boomers started, casual sex and free love became the words of

SEX: Now that I've Captured Your Attention

the hour. We remember women's hot pants, miniskirts, and halters and men's silk shirts, open to the navel, low-riding pants, and gold chains showing off their chest hairs. We all knew people bitten by the crabs, the clap, and various STDs during this promiscuous period of our lives. Now, at our stage of life, STDs have returned and are an issue with some seniors, particularly in the retirement communities and even assisted living facilities.

Sex is natural and fun, but more importantly, it needs to be safe, so we recommend a trip to the doctor or clinic as a precaution. You and your partner should affirm that neither has an STD to share with the other, because sharing toothbrushes and sharing STDs do not have the same outcomes. If you have had casual sex recently, it is critical to make a visit to your doctor. If you haven't had sex in a while, you have a good chance of not having an STD, but better safe than sorry. Those who kept a tight cinch on their chastity belt during their marriage have a lesser chance of having an STD, but check with your doctor for symptoms.

Doctors are sometimes less than excited about talking to someone who is the age of their grandparent about sex, STDs, erectile dysfunction, and female aridity, but don't let their shyness stop you from asking. You may remind them of their own grandparents or their own vulnerability. If you are seeing a PA or NP rather than a doctor, it is fair to ask if they have been trained to discuss sexual issues with their older patients. Many medical personnel have not been trained or educated in sexual activity among senior citizens. Plow ahead, make them blush. Perhaps they will go home shaking their heads, thinking, *OPTD...old people these days.*

The issue of erectile dysfunction has emerged in the past few years and must be either a huge issue or a huge moneymaker for drug companies. Television commercials using virile football stars who take ED drugs are common and embarrass us when our grandchild says, "What's ED, Grandma?" ED is a common male problem after the age of fifty.

Your doctor sat through numerous lectures about it in medical school, but sometimes when the gray-haired patient asks the question, the young medical professional's eyes glaze over, uncomfortable at the thought of Grandpa knowing anything about sex. You should persist, as this is nothing to be ashamed of or shied away from; it is a common problem and has an easy solution.

For women, of course, menopause has granted more sexual freedom, not worrying about a pregnancy, but it also delivers vaginal dryness. A variety of colors, smells, and tastes of vaginal lubricants are on the market, and you can order them online if you feel uncomfortable asking a nosy store clerk where they are. I, Gail, never thought I would say these four words, but now after thinking about the joys of sexual intimacy, all I can say is "TGFM, thank God for menopause."

Sexual intimacy is more than the sex act itself. It means more than touching and kissing and rubbing your partner's back with or without lotions but with care. It means showing your partner that you love them, really love them, enough to take an emotional plunge, giving yourself totally to him or her.

So let us get down to the nitty-gritty. You have exchanged a few texts, phone calls, and dates after your first FDA, and things are moving along quite well. You like him, he likes you, or she likes you and you like her. You've swapped spit a few times and done a bunch of hugs; somebody gave somebody flowers or candy or something else to show affection. You've done the job interview things with each other's kids and/or grandkids, and everybody is aware and confident and feels safe. Most are on board with it too, but we wouldn't take anything for granted yet. People have smiled and said you're a cute couple and how lucky you are, and now somebody, most likely the man, wants to do a sleepover. What to do?

SEX: Now that I've Captured Your Attention

A sleepover? Seriously? We're not talking scout camp; rather it means more necking and smooching and thinking, *What do I do? What have I gotten myself into?* You've gotta take the plunge to go all the way, as we used to say. Yes or no? Or it's a "maybe" working into a yes or no. Somebody is going to say at some point, "It's time to lose our clothes."

You'll know if this is right. Your five senses, plus your mind, body, and soul, will tell you. Don't engage in sex because you are forced into it. Don't engage in sex because you have been intellectually and emotionally intimate with this person—that doesn't mean you must have sex. Engage in sex when you want to dance with your new partner. This may have a variety of paths toward fulfillment, not just the co-mingling of body parts. It is doubtful it will be the same as when we first discovered sex, grappling in the back seat of that '52 Chevy with eager and hurried anticipation and explosive hormones. Now, it is slower and more intimate, talking about what we like, laughing about our trials and errors, feeling each other out, and touching in ways that are gentler and more sincere in our demonstration of love.

The slam-bam-thank-you-ma'am is out, and pillow talk with titillating tickling and beguiling smiles is in. Sex is good, good for us, and is the ultimate intimacy of two people in love.

CHAPTER 17

GETTING ON WITH THE RHYTHM OF LIFE

This book is not about death; it is about life.

We are all meant to love and be loved, and it seems so simple: just laugh, love, and have adventures. However, the entirety of falling in love touches on many things, and like a pebble dropped in water, the ripples bang against facts and require solutions or at least attention. We widowed have fallen in love—pretty nice fact to start with—we both know how precious time is, and we treasure every moment. We control the usage of time, mostly, and don't let it control us. These other ripples, like life's what-ifs, constitute the messy sides of life and deserve attention but not divergence from the primary attention, which is to each other. One of us without the other one leads us back into silence, and we need to remember this perspective in dealing with these puzzles of life.

Frederick Buechner, theologian and author, puts it this way: "One life on this Earth is all we get, whether it is enough or not enough, and the obvious conclusion would seem to be at the very least we are fools if we do not live it as fully and bravely and beautifully as we can." Every day we remind ourselves that the most important thing is to fill out each day as bravely and beautifully as possible. This means starting each day with a text message or phone call when we are apart or a kiss in person and thinking about how to use or enjoy each minute. We live life as though when this minute passes we will never it see again, and we have done all we can do.

Gail's favorite literary hero, Jack Reacher of Lee Child's series, says, "Plan for the worst and hope for the best." Using his logic, one of us could die tomorrow, or we both could live to be ninety-six, almost twenty years from now. The folly of planning for the worst suggests calling the funeral home tomorrow, and the folly of hoping for the best is to borrow against our life insurance and assets, so at age ninety-six we are completely broke (although we enjoyed the ride). Life is somewhere in the middle, and we choose to take some risk in the full enjoyment of each moment. As Hunter S. Thompson says, "Life should not be a journey to the grave with the intention of arriving safely in a well-preserved body. But rather to skid in sideways, chocolate in one hand, wine in the other, body thoroughly worn out and screaming, 'Wahoo, what a ride.'" We tend to take this view of life and enjoy our adventures with gusto, a positive attitude, and our arms around each other.

Our lives continue to charm and excite us, and we take time to thank God for the blessings we see every day. We talk about our spiritual beliefs and agree things are hard to explain without understanding the existence of a higher being. We both agree God does exist and He gives us the strength to continue this trek of life, and for us this belief is both a comfort and a resource. Whether you believe in a higher being or not, many of us are thankful for our beliefs, and this can be a source of peace as you so wish.

When we, Robert and Gail, began our adventure, neither was sure where it would take us, and we struggled with whether we wanted a quick date now and then, a phone/text romance, as we considered the logistical difficulty of living 600 miles apart, or a long-term relationship, laughing as we thought of how long a long-term relationship was when we both had passed the three-quarters-of-a-century mark.

We knew we wanted travel and adventure, an easy conclusion. We craved conversation, both chitter-chatter and more serious discussions. We were excited to talk, to write, and to laugh with the other. We enjoyed touching each other, and yes, we reignited our sexual pleasures. We both had projects and family near our homes that needed attention and didn't want them to suffer. We both came from successful long-term relationships (Gail, fifty-one years, and Robert forty-two years), and both our spouses had passed away after extended and painful diseases. Tom was ill for several years from the effects of Agent Orange from his Vietnam service, and Patty was ill for two years from an untreatable, and terminal, cancer appearing with little or no warning. During those difficult years, we were caregivers first, companions second, and spouses last. We were both widowed for about a year before we met, which had given us time to grieve, settle our affairs, and try to figure out how to get on with life. By chance, we met online, swapping profiles and photos, and eventually swapping spit. Robert knew he was open to a more serious relationship than a one-night stand and wanted a monogamous or committed relationship, perhaps long term. Gail, less certain about any relationship but hungry for laughter and adventure, had been researching one of her *Wrinkly Bits* books and just happened to be online when Robert flipped through the site. He was stopped cold by this silver-haired beauty standing beside a lock, and swiped right, knowing he needed to know more, and the adventure began.

As this love affair grew, first with texting, then long-distance visits, they fell in love and discussed their options, ad nauseum, before she said, "Why don't I sell my house and move to Montana?"

Getting on with the Rhythm of Life

Once Gail agreed to move to Montana, it seemed right, but she added some stipulations. She likes warmer winters, so we are planning some trips to the South in the winter. She wanted garage space for her Lexus and a writing space. She had to concede to allow an open bedroom window, even when the temperature was below freezing, but he bought her an extra down comforter. We learned to love again, share, expect romance, and equally important, to laugh. We looked at adventurous options, like trying new things such as cooking new recipes, gardening, and travel, and sharing as much time as we could with each other, focusing on us. We try to have a new adventure at least twice a week. We have struggled through the job interviews with our children, grandchildren, and some friends. They were unsure at first, but we both got the job as each other's friend and lover. They have slowly but surely come to include each of us as part of their family and realize these two old fogeys love each other and can't do anything about it. We did not try to replace each other's spouse, rather filled in a missing dance step. Now they accept us as a couple, a couple of what, we aren't sure, and of course, we see each other as friends, soul mates, and lovers.

Now we are faced with the realities of life, which are commitment, marriage, or not, adventures, and financial sharing, which includes the legal stuff, like wills, estates, living wills, and our responsibilities to each other as we grow old. After all, we both are highly experienced caregivers. We have talked extensively with our children, grandchildren, lawyers, ministers, and doctors about commitment in a situation such as ours, with a lot of advice and things to consider. All these people, our family and the professionals, have an opinion, a voice, but we are the decision-makers. When end-of-life issues arise, which are inevitable for one or the other of us, these conversations may prove to give the remaining person something to hang on to. We found no easy answer to the final questions, and we can only ask that those involved act with love and honor our commitment to each other.

Consider our children. When our kids were small, we spent time and energy telling them sex before marriage was taboo, naughty, don't do it. They in turn have passed our morality message to their children, who are all in their teens and twenties, some with their own children. But now, we offer a conflicted message saying it is okay for Grandma and Grandpa to omit the wedding vows, but not people under a certain age. They found themselves doing some reconciliation with themselves as well as their children, which probably had a message of "They are old and will die soon anyway, so it's okay," and "Grandma is too old to get pregnant," and "Grandpa is like the old guys on TV with ED." All or most might be true.

One factor in the decision to marry, or not, at our age has to do with financial issues. Income from Social Security, pension plans, and other sources are defined in part by one's marital status, and marriage is a legal change of that status, possibly changing the amount and terms of those assets. Marriage impacts the estates of each and should be part of this financial consideration.

We advise you and your new love to practice due diligence about finances and your proposed marital status. Due diligence includes attorneys, financial advisors, and yes, your family. We decided not to marry, at least at this point, because of various financial complications. We do not hold ourselves out as being married because in some states this can be considered common-law marriage. While we cannot fully explain to our teenage granddaughter why we are allowed to fool around and she isn't, we do have reasons, in addition to being a new adventure.

The financial side doesn't need to be difficult. Each of us has our own resources, but neither of us is a fat cat or a pauper, and we take care of our individual finances. We have an informal agreement to share our common adventure expenses, while retaining control over what we want and don't want to do. We talk about expenses and agree neither is responsible for the other's expenses or debts. We split date expenses, figure out a logical way to pay for trips and other more costly adventures, and keep a good eye on our individual finances. The most important part of financial discussions is being open and honest. If one of us wants or doesn't want something to fit into our budget, we tell each other. The most important thing we have is time. We want to enjoy each minute and not worry so much about finances and forget our most precious commodity, which is time with each other.

An added benefit is that although two can't live as cheaply as one, two can live together more cheaply than two living independently. We moved in together and figured it out, sharing some expenses and keeping others separate. We have cut our expenses enough to continue traveling and go on our date nights.

Two ministers have recommended against our marrying in a non-traditional way, so here we are, living in sin, as we taught our children not to do. We suggested a spiritual blessing ceremony, but it could be interpreted as "holding ourselves out as married," which might put our children at ease, but might complicate things financially. A third minister offered us a blessing, saying our commitment was between us and God, which seems logical, and we think we do this each day. Each person's circumstances are different. Every state is different. Family dynamics are different, and these differences require due diligence. All this is important, but the most important thing is our commitment to each other.

Our doctor sees things differently from our attorneys, and she is less worried about the legal ramifications and reminds us of the importance of a caregiver when medical or emergency issues arise. She has included each of us as the primary who-to-call and decision-maker, should an emergency occur. The doctors understand the "caregiver" role, and in their eyes, this is just as important as the spousal relationship or kinship, should one of us become hurt or ill and need immediate attention. Of course, our children and family will be involved in end-of-life discussions, and this can be a murky issue that depends on medical forms (advanced directives, DNR—Do Not Resuscitate, etc.). We have left clear instructions as to all those actions. Because of our experience and responsibilities with death, we are uniquely qualified to know what happens and what decisions are needed. We tried to ease the burden on the caregiver, with decision-making on health and end of life (including family) being on the caregiver since he/she has the written wishes, but the family still needs to understand they have a grandma or grandpa to bury, wills to probate, and bills to pay. Each situation can be different, so again, check with the state laws and directives; in all cases, keep your immediate family involved and informed as to your wishes. Doctors love having these two geriatric seniors together as helpmates and have offered a variety of supportive ideas for a successful relationship at our stage of life.

So, here we are. It's an adventure. We are having a grand time. We have tried to make our relationship easy for our kids through conversations and actions, but they have not yet experienced making all the decisions that they are certain to confront. When one spouse dies, the widow or widower is faced with a myriad of questions, and the children are bystanders, watching and nodding. When the second spouse dies, however, the kids will have the complicated responsibility of taking care of the death details of their second parent. Until they go through the death of their second parent, it will surprise them how complicated a death can be. Luckily for them, we left written instructions, and it's a good lesson in humility.

Although we are not married, in our minds we are together, committed to each other in a loving relationship. The long-term relationship between us is just that, a solid relationship, regardless of Idaho or Montana law. And, thanks to our willingness to give online dating a go, we are dancing with a new partner, having adventure after adventure, happy in our choices, laughing and smiling a lot, thrilled by the touch of the other, and being crazy in love.

CHAPTER 18

ONLINE DATING GLOSSARY

As with all technology, terminology confuses us, wearing us down, making us feel like we are just now learning a language. And the techno folks are thieves, to boot. Technology has stolen perfectly good words like icon (someone we adore) or back up (what we do to get out of a garage) or virus (something bad making us sick) and replaced or rearranged the definitions, confusing many, especially those of us whose idea of advanced technology is an electric mixer or battery-operated toothbrush or a pet fence that zaps our pet to keep it safe.

Here are a few words that might help you out. If you need more, Google the term or check the *Idiot's Guide to Online Dating Terms and Lingo.*

Term	Definition	Examples	Caution Level
Accomo-dating	When online daters show higher interest about the home than qualities of the person who is listed on the profile, BEWARE.	When was your house built? How long have you lived there? Do you have a mortgage?	EXTREME

Online Dating Glossary

Benching	Like basketball, you are put on hold while they wait for someone else who might be better.	I'm gonna be gone for a couple of days. Don't worry, I'll be back. Just don't find someone else.	Be aware, no caution
Bot	Abbreviated form of robot, meaning the person on the other end of the text might be a machine.	Answers are out of sequence, uncommon punctuation, repetitive questions, you name it.	Caution!
Boost	Boosts are offered to attract attention by altering the profile. It might be good. It might be bad, but undoubtedly, it's going to cost something extra. It may update or increase your status by allowing you to choose a more defined group of online dates.	Your profile might indicate you love adventure, but not say what kind of adventure. Your picture shows a motorcycle, yet you prefer cruising.	none

Breadcrumbing	Leading someone on, just like Hansel and Gretel, leaving little enticements before leaving you cold. Remember high school!	Sending little e-hearts on the texts, but they seem phony	caution
Catch & Release	One-night stand, hooking up for a night of sex with no intention of a commitment	Hey, babe or guy, wanna play catch and release?	Only if it's your thing!
Catfishing and Kittenfishing	A person pretending to be someone they aren't	Like a major medical researcher who says he/she works in a tiny town in Montana. Profile, pictures, and location seem off, not what they should be, and he/she tries to lure you in for sex or money.	BEWARE!
Cuffing Season / Freckling Season	Seasonal romances Cuffing: fall and winter Freckling: spring and summer	Like winter and summer wheat, here today, gone tomorrow	Realize some people do this

Online Dating Glossary

Curve	When someone stands you up for a date, whether IRL or online	Just like high school	Realize some people do this
Cushioning: Also called **Micro-cheating**	Keeping someone on hold when you know you are not interested; flirting with someone you would never go out with	I don't really like her, but I don't want to hurt her	Beware!
Dry Dating	Abstaining from alcohol on dates		Good to know!
DTR: **Define the Relationship**	Are you friends, a couple, or something more? You will know you need to define it when the time comes, but don't define until you are certain.	Important stuff! But be sure!	Good to know!
Emergency Call	Having someone call you and using a code indicating everything is okay or you need help	So sorry, my dog got out and I need to go.	Good idea!
Emojis	Computer-generated pictures that sometimes substitute for words. Most are clever and innocent, but some will make you blush!	Some are nasty. For example, a banana might not mean a potassium-rich fruit.	Ask your grandkids for help.

FDA (First Date Adventure)	Goal of chasing a match	Public place, neutral site for sure!	Follow the rules!
Ghosting	When someone you might care about disappears from your texts or email without a word. If they reappear, it is called **Zombie-ing.**	It happens. There might be a reason, but maybe not.	Good to know!
Groundhogging	Like the movie *Groundhog Day*: using the same words and phrases over and over again with the same thing happening	Alter your approach (but no lies) to address each person individually	No lies!
Haunting or Orbiting	Like a ghost, someone you have rejected keeps reappearing, is lurking in the background. He or she is not worth it!	Even with different names!	BEWARE!
IRL (In Real Life)	When you take your match up a level and decide to meet	Always take caution.	Good for you!

Online Dating Glossary

Love Bombing	A first-time contact showers you with attention and love, but often it fades and/or is a way to lure you into a cult or religious movement.	Hey, beautiful. You have the 3 A's: amazing, attractive, appealing. A trifecta!	BEWARE!
Myers-Briggs	Personality test. It defines who you are with personality traits,	Are you: Introvert or Extrovert Sensing or Intuitive Thinking or Feeling Judging or Perceiving	Fun and interesting to take
Netflix and Chill	A stay-at-home date that sometimes turns into more.	A long time after your FDA, the neutral site date	Eyes wide open!
Profile	An online assessment of you. Every online dating site requires one. What you like and don't like. Be honest, don't exaggerate or lie.	See our workbook for help writing it!	No lies! Can be time-consuming.

Roaching	Sneaky, like cockroaches, a person will say you are the one and only or exaggerate their assets, but say the same thing to a lot of other people too.	Someone with a high school education claiming to be a college professor.	Run away! Another form of deception.
Situationship	Not boyfriend-girlfriend, something more or less. It's complicated because you are in a situationship.	Define the rules between you and your situation person.	Good to know!
Slow-fade	Gradual ghosting, leaving a little at a time	It happens. There might be a reason, but maybe not.	Good to know!
Snack/Full Meal Deal/ Gizzard	**Snack** is a really good-looking person. **Full Meal Deal** is Hot Bananas. Chopped **Gizzard** not for me.	I was looking for a full meal deal but got a snack. Dang.	Good to know!
Stashing or Caspering	You are dating, perhaps in a relationship, but you refuse to let others know.	Is hiding lying?	Good to know!

Online Dating Glossary

Swipe Left	On a mobile phone, swiping toward the left on someone's profile or picture means you reject them…and you can't change your mind.	Not for me!	Not for me, and you can't take another look.
Swipe Right	On a mobile phone, swiping toward the right on someone's profile or picture means you like them. If they like you, they'll send you a heart or something.	I like, I'm interested!	You can take another look.
Super Swiping	Swiping up (on some sites) means you are really interested; in other words, I really like him or her!		Get ready for hot flashes.
Submarining	This happens when someone pays attention to you, disappears, then suddenly reappears.	Like Ghosting	Ask questions to find out why!
Thicc	A new word for voluptuous with body curves	You have a thicc bod!	Maybe a compliment.

Thirsty	If you are desperate for sex, say you are thirsty.	Really? I just wanted a glass of water.	Good to know!
Tuning/ Negging	**Tuning:** flirting stage, but sometimes they are phony, meaningless compliments **Negging:** similar to tuning, using negative comments or sarcasm	I've never seen anyone with bluer eyes. Ooh la la. Don't you look fab? I would never have the courage to wear a shirt that color.	Caution… can be insincere, build you up, then drop you like a sack of rocks.
Voicefishing	Someone using a fake accent or profile to reel someone in	*Il ne faut rien laisser au hasard*	Form of lying.
Wokefishing	People pretend to be progressive or conservative to learn about or persuade other's political views on social issues.		Form of lying or manipulation.

CHAPTER 19

Play-by-Play Book

This book is meant to be a guide to your early exposure to online dating. The Play-by-Play Book is a self-examination and will spur you to think about these topics before you are under the pressure of an actual date. It will help you to think about those first few minutes, hours, or days you spend getting to know someone. Of course, we have all met a new person and dug into a quick conversation, but it is helpful to ponder our path if we are thinking of going beyond a cup of coffee or a fantastic meal or going on a cruise.

No one will see these, except you, and they may spur other questions that you want to ask yourself. Have fun with them, and we hope you find them useful.

Many people receive dozens of "matches," and the last section of this Play-by-Play Book will help you keep track of your suitors. But remember, don't lie!

Day-to-Day Living

Yes	No	Things I love to do:	Comment
		laughing	
		taking risks	
		snacking	
		meeting new people	
		talking	
		sprinkling profanity	
		wearing perfume/cologne	
		traveling	
		socializing at parties or other gatherings	
		being seen with someone	
		staying at home	

Physical Intimacy/Romance

Yes	No	What's important to me:	Comment
		kissing	
		holding hands	
		being hugged	
		being touched	
		being massaged	
		smooching/necking	
		talking about sex	
		telling secrets	
		answering questions about sex	
		pillow talk	
		romance	
		giving or getting presents	
		cuddling	
		that no means no	
		that my boundaries are clear	

Activities

Yes	No	Things I love to do:	Comment
		outdoor activities	
		indoor activities	
		gambling	
		playing cards	
		cleaning and cooking	
		watching TV	
		attending sporting/music events	
		dancing	
		doing things alone	
		playing with pets	
		recreational shopping	
		going places	
		camping	
		fishing/hunting	
		Others?	

Preferences

Yes	No	I would prefer my friend and partner to be	Comment
		the same race as I am	
		of the same ethnic background as I am	
		the same education level as I am	
		slim and trim	
		one who dresses stylishly	
		of the same religious faith	
		a church attender	
		retired	
		punctual	
		politically aligned	
		politically active	
		at the same monetary level as I am	

Questions to Think About

Yes	No	It would bother me if my date	Comment
		were more/less sophisticated than I	
		had sparse hair or none	
		takes a bite of food from my plate	
		has tattoos I didn't know about	
		is extraordinarily beautiful or handsome and I consider myself a plain Jane or John	
		has visible tattoos	
		plunks down a handful of pills on the table before we start to eat	
		is an obvious turn-off	
		has hearing aids, but asks "what?" or gives an off-subject answer	
		forgot his or her wallet, but the date was set up to go Dutch	
		shows up high or drunk	
		wears a wedding ring	
		has personal hygiene issues	

CHAPTER 20

Let's Go Hunting: A Workbook

Dating Site: _____ Date, first contact: _____
Username: _____
Password: _____
Email Used: _____
Other: _____

Dating Site: _____ Date, first contact: _____
Username: _____
Password: _____
Email Used: _____
Other: _____

Dating Site: _____ Date, first contact: _____
Username: _____
Password: _____
Email Used: _____
Other: _____

Loving Again

Dating Site: _____ Date, first contact: _____
Username: _____
Password: _____
Email Used: _____
Other: _____

Dating Site: _____ Date, first contact: _____
Username: _____
Password: _____
Email Used: _____
Other: _____

Dating Site: _____ Date, first contact: _____
Username: _____
Password: _____
Email Used: _____
Other: _____

Dating Site: _____ Date, first contact: _____
Username: _____
Password: _____
Email Used: _____
Other: _____

Dating Site: _____ Date, first contact: _____
Username: _____
Password: _____
Email Used: _____
Other: _____

Let's Go Hunting: Who Do I Like?

Name _____ Date _____
Age _____ Occupation _____
Location _____
Sent me smile, heart, thumbs-up _____
Profile rating: *Liked   Didn't like   Ooh-la-la!* _____
Picture rating: *1   2   3   4   Hot bananas!*
First impression: *Never in a million years   Why me?   Blah   Oh, Baby!*
Comments: _____
_____
_____

***

Name _____ Date _____
Age _____ Occupation _____
Location _____
Sent me smile, heart, thumbs-up _____
Profile rating: *Liked   Didn't like   Ooh-la-la!* _____
Picture rating: *1   2   3   4   Hot bananas!*
First impression: *Never in a million years   Why me?   Blah   Oh, Baby!*
Comments: _____
_____
_____

LOVING AGAIN

Name _____ Date _____
Age _____ Occupation _____
Location _____
Sent me smile, heart, thumbs-up _____
Profile rating: *Liked   Didn't like   Ooh-la-la!* _____
Picture rating: *1   2   3   4   Hot bananas!*
First impression: *Never in a million years   Why me?   Blah   Oh, Baby!*
Comments: _____
_____
_____

***

Name _____ Date _____
Age _____ Occupation _____
Location _____
Sent me smile, heart, thumbs-up _____
Profile rating: *Liked   Didn't like   Ooh-la-la!* _____
Picture rating: *1   2   3   4   Hot bananas!*
First impression: *Never in a million years   Why me?   Blah   Oh, Baby!*
Comments: _____
_____
_____

Let's Go Hunting: A Workbook

Name _____ Date _____
Age _____ Occupation _____
Location _____
Sent me smile, heart, thumbs-up _____
Profile rating: *Liked   Didn't like   Ooh-la-la!* _____
Picture rating: *1 2 3 4 Hot bananas!*
First impression: *Never in a million years   Why me?   Blah   Oh, Baby!*
Comments: _____
_____
_____

***

Name _____ Date _____
Age _____ Occupation _____
Location _____
Sent me smile, heart, thumbs-up _____
Profile rating: *Liked   Didn't like   Ooh-la-la!* _____
Picture rating: *1 2 3 4 Hot bananas!*
First impression: *Never in a million years   Why me?   Blah   Oh, Baby!*
Comments: _____
_____
_____

LOVING AGAIN

Name _____ Date _____
Age _____ Occupation _____
Location _____
Sent me smile, heart, thumbs-up _____
Profile rating: *Liked   Didn't like   Ooh-la-la!* _____
Picture rating: *1   2   3   4   Hot bananas!*
First impression: *Never in a million years   Why me?   Blah   Oh, Baby!*
Comments: _____
_____
_____

***

Name _____ Date _____
Age _____ Occupation _____
Location _____
Sent me smile, heart, thumbs-up _____
Profile rating: *Liked   Didn't like   Ooh-la-la!* _____
Picture rating: *1   2   3   4   Hot bananas!*
First impression: *Never in a million years   Why me?   Blah   Oh, Baby!*
Comments: _____
_____
_____

Let's Go Hunting: A Workbook

Name_____ Date_____
Age _____ Occupation _____
Location _____
Sent me smile, heart, thumbs-up_____
Profile rating: *Liked   Didn't like   Ooh-la-la!*_____
Picture rating: *1 2 3 4   Hot bananas!*
First impression: *Never in a million years   Why me?   Blah   Oh, Baby!*
Comments: _____
_____
_____

***

Name_____ Date_____
Age _____ Occupation _____
Location _____
Sent me smile, heart, thumbs-up_____
Profile rating: *Liked   Didn't like   Ooh-la-la!*_____
Picture rating: *1 2 3 4   Hot bananas!*
First impression: *Never in a million years   Why me?   Blah   Oh, Baby!*
Comments: _____
_____
_____

Loving Again

Name _____ Date _____
Age _____ Occupation _____
Location _____
Sent me smile, heart, thumbs-up _____
Profile rating: *Liked   Didn't like   Ooh-la-la!* _____
Picture rating: *1   2   3   4   Hot bananas!*
First impression: *Never in a million years   Why me?   Blah   Oh, Baby!*
Comments: _____
_____
_____

***

Name _____ Date _____
Age _____ Occupation _____
Location _____
Sent me smile, heart, thumbs-up _____
Profile rating: *Liked   Didn't like   Ooh-la-la!* _____
Picture rating: *1   2   3   4   Hot bananas!*
First impression: *Never in a million years   Why me?   Blah   Oh, Baby!*
Comments: _____
_____
_____

Let's Go Hunting: A Workbook

Name_____Date_____
Age _____Occupation _____
Location _____
Sent me smile, heart, thumbs-up_____
Profile rating: *Liked   Didn't like   Ooh-la-la!*_____
Picture rating: *1 2 3 4   Hot bananas!*
First impression: *Never in a million years   Why me? Blah   Oh, Baby!*
Comments: _____
_____
_____

***

Name_____Date_____
Age _____Occupation _____
Location _____
Sent me smile, heart, thumbs-up_____
Profile rating: *Liked   Didn't like   Ooh-la-la!*_____
Picture rating: *1 2 3 4   Hot bananas!*
First impression: *Never in a million years   Why me? Blah   Oh, Baby!*
Comments: _____
_____
_____

LOVING AGAIN

Name _____ Date _____
Age _____ Occupation _____
Location _____
Sent me smile, heart, thumbs-up _____
Profile rating: *Liked   Didn't like   Ooh-la-la!* _____
Picture rating: *1   2   3   4   Hot bananas!*
First impression: *Never in a million years   Why me?   Blah   Oh, Baby!*
Comments: _____
_____
_____

***

Name _____ Date _____
Age _____ Occupation _____
Location _____
Sent me smile, heart, thumbs-up _____
Profile rating: *Liked   Didn't like   Ooh-la-la!* _____
Picture rating: *1   2   3   4   Hot bananas!*
First impression: *Never in a million years   Why me?   Blah   Oh, Baby!*
Comments: _____
_____
_____

Let's Go Hunting: A Workbook

Name _____ Date _____
Age _____ Occupation _____
Location _____
Sent me smile, heart, thumbs-up _____
Profile rating: *Liked   Didn't like   Ooh-la-la!* _____
Picture rating: *1   2   3   4   Hot bananas!*
First impression: *Never in a million years   Why me?   Blah   Oh, Baby!*
Comments: _____
_____
_____

***

Name _____ Date _____
Age _____ Occupation _____
Location _____
Sent me smile, heart, thumbs-up _____
Profile rating: *Liked   Didn't like   Ooh-la-la!* _____
Picture rating: *1   2   3   4   Hot bananas!*
First impression: *Never in a million years   Why me?   Blah   Oh, Baby!*
Comments: _____
_____
_____

Loving Again

Name _____ Date _____
Age _____ Occupation _____
Location _____
Sent me smile, heart, thumbs-up _____
Profile rating: *Liked   Didn't like   Ooh-la-la!* _____
Picture rating: *1   2   3   4   Hot bananas!*
First impression: *Never in a million years   Why me?   Blah   Oh, Baby!*
Comments: _____
_____
_____

***

Name _____ Date _____
Age _____ Occupation _____
Location _____
Sent me smile, heart, thumbs-up _____
Profile rating: *Liked   Didn't like   Ooh-la-la!* _____
Picture rating: *1   2   3   4   Hot bananas!*
First impression: *Never in a million years   Why me?   Blah   Oh, Baby!*
Comments: _____
_____
_____

WORKS CITED

Adams, Patch. *Gesundheit!: Bringing Good Health to You, the Medical System.* Gesundheit Institute. 1998.

Anderer, John. Get a Hold of Yourself. *Nature Aging.* January 17, 2023.

Anderson, Monica., Vogels, Emily A., Turner, Erica. *Pew Research.* "The Virtues and Downsides of Online Dating." 2020. https://www.pewresearch.org/internet/2020/02/06/the-virtues-and-downsides-of-online-dating/

Baskett, Clint. Facebook. 2022.

Bestcompany.com. https://bestcompany.com/online-dating

Better Aging. "The Benefits of Sexual Activity On Memory And Brain Health." May 24, 2020. https://www.betteraging.com

Bortz, Walter M. *We Live Too Short and Die Too Long.* Bantam. 1992.

Buck, Pearl. Unknown source. Unknown date.

Buechner, Frederick. Theologian and Author. https://www.frederickbuechner.com/

Carr, Dawn, PhD. Florida State University. "Widowhood." Institute for Successful Longevity. 2017.

Child, Lee. *Jack Reacher Series.*

ChristianMingle. https://www.ChristianMingle.com

Cole, Steve, PhD. Social Genomics Core Laboratory at the University of California, Los Angeles NIH (News in Health). April 23, 2019.

Consumeraffairs.com. "Our Time reviews." 2022.

Cushman, Gail. "Lessons on Loneliness from Small Town America." gailcushman.com. October 28, 2022.

Datingadvice.com. https://www.datingadvice.com /

eHarmony. https://www.eHarmony.com

EliteSingles. https://www.EliteSingles.com

ExploringYourMind.com. "Making Love Is Also Laughing Together." September 27, 2016. https://exploringyourmind.com/making-love-also-laughing-together/

FarmersOnly. https://www.FarmersOnly.com

Federal Bureau of Investigation. Internet Crime Complaint Center. . https://www.ic3.gov

Fields, Tara. *The Love Fix*. William Morrow Paperbacks. 2015.

Frost, Robert. https://www.poetryfoundation.org/poems/44272/the-road-not-taken

Gonsalves, Kelly. "45 Small Ways To Be More Romantic In Your Relationships." 2021. https://www.mindbodygreen.com/articles/how-to-be-romantic

Jones, Alexis. *Women's Health*. "How to Flirt with ALL the Confidence." May 26, 2020. https://www.womenshealthmag.com/relationships/a32602758/how-to-flirt-tips/

Jung, Erica. *Fear of Flying*. Holt, Rinehart, and Winston. 1973

Kavanaugh, Molly. *Kendal at Oberlin* "The Myths About Sexuality and Aging." March 16, 2022.

Kearnes, Michele. *Joy Returns*. 2012-2022. https://joyreturns.com

Kleinplatz, Peggy J. PhD. *Magnificent Sex: Lessons from Extraordinary Lovers*. 2020.

Lowbrow, Yeoman. *The Decade of Decadence: A Quick Look at the Sexual Revolution*. March 2, 2015. https://flashbak.com/the-decade-of-decadence-a-quick-look-at-the-sexual-revolution-29469/

Marchant, Natalie L. Repetitive Negative Thinking. *Alzheimer's & Dementia*. June 7, 2020.

Match. https://www.Match.com

Matchmaking.com (out of service at this writing)

Max, Tucker. *I Hope They Serve Beer in Hell*. Rebel Base Books. Los Angeles. 2009.

Works Cited

Meltzer, Marisa. *Consumer Reports*. "Online Dating: Match Me If You Can." December 29, 2016.

National Institute on Aging. "Social isolation, loneliness in older people pose health risks." April 23, 2019. https://www.ncbi.nlm.nih.gov/pmc/articles/PMC7437541/

Norton, Amy. *Health Day*. "Sex Still Matters to Many Seniors." May 2013. https://www.webmd.com/healthy-aging/news/20180503/sex-still-matters-to-many-seniors-survey-finds

OurTime. https://www.OurTime.com

The Power of Positivity. 8 Signs of Loneliness and Depression You Should Never Ignore. https://www.powerofpositivity.com/. December 2022.

Richardson, Peter S. *Savage Journey*. U of California Press. 2022.

Righteous Brothers. "Unchained Melody." 1965.

Rindfleisch, J. Adam. VA Office of Patient Centered Care and Cultural Transformations. "The Healing Benefits of Humor and Laughter." 2018. https://www.va.gov/WholeHealthLibrary/tools/healing-benefits-humor-laughter.asp

SilverSingles. https://www.SilverSingles.com

Sleepless in Seattle. Movie. 1993.

Statista.com. "Marital Status of the United States Population in 2021, by Sex." 2021

Stein, Loren. *Health Day*, "Sex and Seniors: The 70-Year Itch." June 12, 2021. https://consumer.healthday.com/encyclopedia/aging-1/misc-aging-news-10/sex-and-seniors-the-70-year-itch-647575.html .

Stewart, Potter, Supreme Court Justice. *Nico Jacobellis v. Ohio* 1964.

Thompson, Hunter S. AZ Quotes. https://www.azquotes.com/

U.S. Census Bureau, Administration for Community Living; Administration on Aging. "Profile of Older Americans." 2017 and 2021. https://acl.gov/sites/default/files/Aging%20and%20Disability%20in%20America/2020ProfileOlderAmericans.Final_.pdf

U.S. Department of Health and Human Services. "Profile of Older Americans." 2020.

Vatsyayana. *Kama Sutra*. Translated from Sanskrit 400 B.C. 1883.

Vida Select. *The Idiot's Guide to Online Dating and Lingo*. 2022. https://www.vidaselect.com/matchmaking-service/

Wikipedia. Dominance of online dating. "How Heterosexual Couples Have Met, Data from 2009 and 2017." November 2021.

Zwilling, Martin. *Forbes Magazine*. "How Many More Online Dating Sites Do We Need?" 2013.

ABOUT THE AUTHORS

Gail, age 76, B.S., M.A., Ed. Sp., is an Idaho writer, a Marine Corps officer, and former school principal and superintendent. She writes romantic comedies, mysteries, and blogs. Robert, age 77, is a Montana blog writer and rancher who retired as an aviation management professional, leadership consultant trainer, and expert witness.

Gail writes romantic comedies. Her *Wrinkly Bits* series tells stories of seniors over sixty-five who decide to kick up their heels and have romantic adventures. They are self-published but she has sold about two-thousand books in fourteen months. She has written five additional books which are unpublished. She also writes humorous blogs called "Wrinkly Bits" twice weekly, and Robert writes in conjunction with her blogs, as Cowboy Bob, a lonesome, love-struck cowboy in Montana

GailCushman.com is a webpage for information about the co-authors and showcases the blogs, their books and the news about the authors.

Loving Again

Made in the USA
Monee, IL
30 December 2024